W9-ACV-801

MAKING A GOOD CHURCH GREAT

Steve Sjogren once again bucks the culture, this time debunking the idea that churches must show "amazingly great excellence" in all they do. He invites leaders to follow a different set of standards—such as being known for simplicity, generosity and outreach. He shows what it takes to make a good church truly great.

WARREN BIRD
Research Director, Leadership Network
Co-author of *Multi-Site Church Roadtrip*

Steve Sjogren makes the inaccessible accessible. Drawing on firsthand and deeply personal experience (I know because I've cleaned toilets with him), Steve leads you step by step through the lessons he's learned planting one of the most influential churches in America.

JIM HENDERSON
Author of *Evangelism Without Additives, Jim and Casper Go to Church* and *The Outsider Interviews*

Knowing Steve Sjogren for more than 30 years has given me a credible perspective concerning his life and ministry. His innovative and sometimes unorthodox methods to reach the unchurched have always been motivated by an authentic passion to serve the Lord. Through the hardships and struggles of life, Steve has tenaciously persevered in this lifelong quest to build the Kingdom.

TRI ROBINSON
Author of *Saving God's Green Earth*
Senior Pastor of Vineyard Boise, Idaho

Steve Sjogren always makes me think . . . and this book is no different. As I read *Making a Good Church Great*, I found myself nodding yes sometimes, being stretched to think differently at others, and more than once thinking, *I wish I had said that!* Grab a cup of coffee and your notepad as you read this book . . . Steve is about to challenge us all to lead great churches.

NELSON SEARCY
Lead Pastor of The Journey Church (New York City)
Founder of www.ChurchLeaderInsights.com

This book hits the nail on the head. No church is a great church unless it has great transformed lives. Thanks, Steve, for painting a great picture of what a church—any church—can be.

ELMER L. TOWNS
Dean of the School of Theology, Liberty University
Author of *What's Right With the Church*

In *Making a Good Church Great*, Steve Sjogren, the "father of servant evangelism," offers surprising thoughts on what makes churches healthy and effective. His genuine mix of passion, head-tilting ideas and spiritual pragmatism will challenge conventional assumptions and will cause you to rethink current "church-effectiveness" strategies. I'm convinced that we need more innovators and confront-the-status-quo practitioners like Steve. His stories and hard-earned experiences are guaranteed to get your neurons firing!

DAVE WORKMAN
Author of *The Outward Focused Life: Becoming a Servant in a Serve-Me World*

Steve Sjogren

MAKING A
GOOD
CHURCH
GREAT

Regal

From Gospel Light
Ventura, California, U.S.A.

Becoming a Community
God Calls His Home

Published by Regal
From Gospel Light
Ventura, California, U.S.A.
www.regalbooks.com
Printed in the U.S.A.

Previously published as *The Perfectly Imperfect Church* by
Flagship Church Resources in 2002.

Library of Congress Cataloging-in-Publication Data
Sjogren, Steve, 1955-
Making a good church great : becoming a community God calls his home /
Steve Sjogren.
p. cm.
ISBN 978-0-8307-4662-0 (hard cover)
1. Church. I. Title.
BV600.3.S56 2010
254'.5—dc22
2009037675

1 2 3 4 5 6 7 8 9 10 / 15 14 13 12 11 10

Rights for publishing this book outside the U.S.A. or in non-English languages are
administered by Gospel Light Worldwide, an international not-for-profit ministry.
For additional information, please visit www.glww.org, email info@glww.org, or write
to Gospel Light Worldwide, 1957 Eastman Avenue, Ventura, CA 93003, U.S.A.

*This book is dedicated to Kenn Gulliksen, my pastor
when I started out in ministry and my mentor. Among other things,
Kenn's model and priority of God's presence being the key
to greatness for the Kingdom is what kept me pressing forward,
upward and outward. While the Vineyard Christian Fellowship
that Kenn led in West Los Angeles was never listed as one of the
fastest-growing or largest churches, God was present,
lives were transformed the Kingdom grew and Kenn was
pastor of a truly great church.*

Contents

Once we experience the actual presence of God, we lose all interest in cheap Christianity with its bells and whistles.

A. W. TOZER

Preface

True greatness is not a fad, nor is it a bestseller. It is not the number of people at church on Sunday morning or the number of television stations that broadcast your message. It is not even the number of decisions for Christ or healings claimed in the name of Jesus.

Nothing is wrong with selling books, preaching the gospel or praying for the sick. But if you want to know if you have a great church, you need to stop for a moment and look around. Look at the people who attend. Do you see changed lives? Watch as they worship. Is God present? Is He tangibly present, and not just words on a big screen?

Greatness comes when God is there, right beside you, inside you, all around you, and His love flows out from you whether you have 20 people or 20,000 people in your church. When we move from the spectacle to the miracle of transforming lives and communities, and pass the test of time, then and only then have we taken a step toward true greatness.

In this book, I present some ideas that I have learned over the years as a church member, planter, pastor and consultant. This isn't an ultimate how-to book or theological treatise, but a practical package of ideas that can help move your church from good to great.

Introduction

THE AHA! EXPERIENCE

BECOMING GREAT FOR THE KINGDOM

Sometimes I see things for the first time after a thousand glances. That happened to me while I was observing and analyzing the DNA and workings of one particular church.

As a friendly consultant, I walked into First Community Church so often that I quit keeping track of my time. Leadership told me repeatedly that their goal was to "become something great for God." But after being with them for more than 100 hours, I concluded they were aspiring to a level of imagined fame that in reality they were not destined to become.

The pastor was a good guy, though his gifting was not off the charts. He could deliver a message well enough, but I suspected that he would never become well known as an author or speaker. I was fairly certain I would not be seeing him on Christian TV anytime soon. The church was doing outreach programs in the community that were competent but not outstanding. The people genuinely loved one another—that was clear. Their worship times were genuine. When I was with them, even though I didn't know all the songs, I could feel the presence of the Lord clearly enough.

People felt a sense of safety in the midst of their gatherings, on multiple levels, and that feeling of safety allowed them to bring their friends to services. Safety was one of the leading causes for the numerical growth they had seen. They were fun people to be with. A sense of care seemed to abound in their small groups.

People seemed to often understand intuitively what it took for a church to grow, so the atmosphere they created fostered expansion. Generosity marked the way these folks related to the people outside their ranks. They told me they gave up long ago on arguing over small doctrinal issues. Their motto was to keep to the "main and the plain." One of their greatest joys was to promote other churches in the city in various ways. They were always generous in the way they related to others regardless of the issue or the way in which matters popped up.

Thinking about all these factors and this church, I had what Norwegians call an *aha opplevelse* (a-ha up-level-suh), which can be roughly translated as an "aha! experience," although it means much more than how Americans tend to use that word. It means seeing something with new eyes. It means that someone gets so excited upon getting in touch with an idea that he jumps up and down and begins to march around the room with virtually unbridled enthusiasm, shouting "WOW! Now that was different. Now I get it. This part of life suddenly makes sense to me."

I had several aha! experiences with these people. My interactions with them led me to see more clearly than I had ever seen before. What I learned caused me to revise my definition of what makes a good church great and to go back to some of the spiritual principles I flourished in when I led my first small-group Bible study many years ago.

Aha! #1:
Imperfect Can Be Perfect

First Community Church wasn't called to be spectacular by the narrow definition that's been drummed into my head by untold numbers of books, articles and word-of-mouth myths. People in this congregation were called to be themselves.

I had it in my head that there was just one sort of church out there that one would want to aspire to be in the world of churches. I had previously thought that in order to make a difference a church had to be in the top 1 percent of churches—

a church with at least 1,000 people in regular attendance. Yet this church was doing well in virtually every measurable respect other than not being large numerically speaking. After years of being together, they measured about 400 in number—no small feat, all things considered.

My aha! moment brought the realization that this church was doing great things for the cause of Christ at its current size. The church wasn't perfect, but it was a great church by all measurable aspects.

We make a mistake when we evaluate a church's success strictly in terms of numerical growth. Alan Roxburgh described this misplaced emphasis in his book *Missionary Congregation, Leadership and Liminality*. He wrote, "Numerical growth is the talisman of our ecclesiological health . . . technique is the primary method for reestablishing the church's place in the culture. God is but a legitimating footnote of ecclesiology . . . the Harvard School of Business, Faith Popcorn, and George Barna are the contemporary saints."[1]

Aha! #2
Bigger Is Not Always Better,
Nor Is It More Effective

Not so long ago, the so-called mega-churches were all the rage. During the 1980s and '90s, the burning question in church leadership circles was "How can I grow a giant-sized church?" Recently, the mega-church trend is fading.

We have seen churches grow in record numbers during the past 20 years, but history has shown that church health does not come hand in hand with numerical growth. The burning issue for the next few decades, it seems, will be church health.

In spite of a few highly visible churches, the mega-church is going to become more and more of a dinosaur on the church landscape in America. The primary reason for this is the simple fact that as attendance numbers pass the thousand mark, church health is increasingly difficult to maintain.

Aha! #3
Church Health Is Measured by Competence, Not Competition

How can you know whether or not you're doing what you should be doing? Scan through the pages of magazines such as *Charisma, Ministries Today* or most issues of *Christianity Today* and you will find a bipolar message. Mixed in with the help the magazines offer are lots of subliminal messages, including:

- If your church counts, it will be large—very large, in fact.

- If you count as a leader, you will look like, talk like, teach like and lead like the guys who are getting national attention (i.e., very white teeth, a big smile, striking Italian suit).

- If you want to go anywhere with your church, you'd better get yourself to the "happening" conferences where you can learn to emulate those lead guys who seem to do this without even having to give it a thought. In fact, you need to make one of these magical treks that seem to be able to cause church growth to occur without much of a second thought about it.

The underlying message is that the more you're like the pastors of large churches, the more confident you can be that you're doing what you should and you are following God's will. However, imitating leaders of large churches—striving to have the most welcoming smile, the most inspiring speeches and, of course, the most gigantic numbers—can cause pastors to become competitive.

Action is a good thing, but over-stimulation and a lack of direction can become distracting. They can resemble an overdose of caffeine. We can become people with a horrid case of the jitters—where all action seems to be good action. But that is rarely true. We need to be directing our actions in intelligent paths. Too much of a good thing can drive us to distraction. I've been an avid coffee drinker for years; however, I've learned recently that it is possible to drink a lethal dose of java (suicide by Starbucks?). The thought is staggering. If a person who weighs about 150 pounds consumed some 80 cups of coffee, in a short time, some really bad things would happen to his or her heart, kidneys and liver.

We don't need an outside stimulant to do the work of the Holy Spirit. He is ready, willing and able to fill us with His power and change the world. (I wonder if some of the leaders of the mega-churches who have been presented to us as models are on major doses of caffeine? Just a thought. But some of the smiles I see in Christian magazines seem to be a little jittery.)

More than a few times I have walked away de-energized from leadership conferences that were supposed to be encouraging and uplifting. Typically, I spent the first day of the conference listening to a pastor of a gigantic church who was trying to sincerely convince me that he was just like me. Then he would go into his approach to church life, an approach that had spawned his many books on the topic. By the second day, I wasn't feeling so good about the conference, about myself or my ministry, for that matter. Then it hit me: I wasn't listening to a regular person. This was a Superman! No wonder I was discouraged. I couldn't compete. This person was so over-the-top that it was amazing, and it was impossible to relate, in any sense of the word. I could never compete with this person. There was little if anything this person did that intersected with my life, because he was just that extraordinary.

While conferences and publications offer helpful advice, unintended messages can damage the souls of their followers. The subtle messages they offer can lead to the conclusion that we are involved in a competition to outdo one another to become bigger, faster, more.

In *Making a Good Church Great*, I describe what I call the great church, because a church doesn't have to fit the reigning definition of perfect in order to have a powerful ministry. I tend to interchange the term "great church" with "pretty good church" throughout the book. The second term is one that I lifted from psychologist Abraham Maslow and his teaching of the hierarchy of human needs. He observed that we all have basic human needs that must be met in order to survive. These are needs for food, water and shelter. Once the basic needs are met, we have social and emotional needs, such as the need to belong. People exist at all levels of the hierarchy of human needs that Maslow describes in the shape of a pyramid.

At the top of the pyramid are the needs of the few hearty souls Maslow calls the "self-actualized." With all their needs having been met, these people no longer crave affirmation.

Instead of needing something, they give away affirmation to others. In Maslow's model and grid, the parents who qualify as the best parents are what he calls the "good enough" parents. Good enough parents are good listeners and affirmers, and they seek to help their children become successful in whatever field of interest those children have in their hearts to pursue. Good enough parents are not competitive; they are affirming of the journey that each child takes up.

Maslow's description of the good enough parent could also be extended to a description of the good enough church. Yet, today's overemphasis on the pursuit of excellence has led to a highly competitive attitude among churches and church leaders that has not been matched in recent history. Dr. Maslow wouldn't have been surprised. He found that overly aggressive behavior indicates that a person is not progressed very far on the emotional trek of life. For the church, I would interpret that to mean that the goal is to be better than the church down the street or to build a church larger than one across town. The church world beckons us to do more, be better, work faster than the guys down the street. But we don't have to fall into that trap. We don't have to be perfect. We're okay being a great church.

Aha! #4
The Best Churches May Not Necessarily Be the Most Visible Ones

There exists an unofficial "CPC" ("church politically correct") thought in the church world. I don't want to sound like a conspiracy theorist, but perhaps there is even an agenda (or at least a tendency based on comfort and familiarity) in the popular

Christian media to promote certain groups, congregations and individual heroes—to lionize them while ignoring others who are doing a great job and usually working in the trenches to a degree that would warm Mother Teresa's heart . . . and, no doubt, God's heart. Look at church media news; with few exceptions, the same churches and leaders are talked about over and over again.

The church world is very slow to gain and then slow to release its heroes, once they have been installed. We even want to overlook blemishes and some big blunders that God would call sin, holding tightly to what we have come to idolize. Ouch. We are slow to recognize when in our hearts and our actions we have placed a leader, a church, a cause, a project, a revival, a crusade or a movement ahead of God.

So often it's impossible to gain real encouragement from the churches being presented as super-successful because they are so distinctive. In spite of good intentions, many of those discouraging leadership conferences are sponsored by the mega-churches. After seeing the perfect execution of the apparently flawless church, conference attendees leave thinking, "Hey, we'll never get there. We'll never raise that much money. We'll never recruit that many gifted leaders. Our people will never respond like these people. Bottom line, this will never work at our place."

The best churches in America vary significantly from one another. They are sometimes large; they are sometimes significantly smaller. Often they are medium-sized (with weekend attendance of 300 to 500 people). They are usually not easy to explain, and their nonconformance with accepted practices may even seem iconoclastic. The Christian media isn't entirely comfortable with the leadership of these churches, because many of the leaders aren't exactly like us.

T. D. Jakes, who shot up out of nowhere to national prominence, is an interesting example. The multiethnic church The Potter's House, which he founded in Dallas in 1996, has more than 30,000 members and is growing rapidly. The popular Christian media doesn't know what to do with Jakes. I've heard people ask, "Who's the next Billy Graham?" I wonder if it is Jakes myself. Like Graham, he came out of nowhere into sudden national prominence in spite of having few resources. His success is virtually impossible to explain without a large God element.

Based on the significance of my four aha! experiences, I have identified four categories of churches. As you'll see, they vary in health and effectiveness. The very last of the two healthy church models described is the "great church" whose characteristics I weaved into a description of the church in the opening paragraphs of this introduction. Before we get to that model, let's take a look at the struggling church.

Four Kinds of Churches

1. The Struggling Church

Typical of the vast majority of churches in America is a church with a weekend attendance of fewer than 200. Like it or not, it takes at least 200 people to support a church and keep it solvent financially and, in terms of energy, to keep it keeping on. For a minimally staffed, full-service church with a full-time pastor, a part-time assistant and a part-time youth person, it takes the financial wherewithal of at least 200 people to support it.

Unfortunately, this is also the size that leads to the maximum amount of utter frustration in a local church. When we are focused upon the notion that we are giving ourselves away in an outwardly focused way such as this, we are likely to burn out if we stay at this size for long. Both on paper and in real-life experience, as I have intersected with many hundreds of pastors in the trenches of day-to-day church life, I have discovered that this size is the maximum level of frustration and the minimum level of satisfaction in ministry. Yet, as far as the average mean size of churches in America, the 200-attendance level is very close to the most commonly occurring size congregation across the country. Thus, most people belong to a church that is stuck in the doldrums of enormous frustration among the leadership, who are experiencing little satisfaction as far as ministry outcome goes.

What is a person in this situation to do? What is a minister to do if he is in the midst of a titanic struggle such as this? In a manner of speaking, it would be easier if the church were to either implode and go away or take off and become something much more significant in terms of size.

Saying that a church is struggling because of its size is no doubt offensive to some. I don't mean to be disrespectful of the struggling church. I've been the leader of three of them for a prolonged time period and know the challenges involved. Struggling churches are difficult to be a part of and challenging to run; they are not large enough to adequately do quality worship, childcare, team ministry, or encourage an active lay leadership.

Some years ago, a survey conducted by the Barna research team found that 40 percent of 3,764 Protestant churches contacted had no one answering the phone.[2] On top of that, almost half of those churches (44 percent) didn't even have an answering machine, something that would go a long way toward saying to the public, "We're interested in you and your call." These statistics tell a lot about a struggling church and how difficult it is to keep the fires going.

Being a veteran leader of struggling churches, I know about the emotional and spiritual stress that is present in these organizations. Every day is a challenge just to keep on going. Here are a few specific stressors:

- The goal is to survive from week to week, from offering to offering.
- One family leaving creates a crisis in momentum.
- Constant effort is required to keep everything afloat.
- Leading is not fun after a time.
- Involvement for a long period of time is unhealthy at every level for everyone involved.

Being a struggling church is much like being a part of a sailboat crew that is not quite large enough to make a safe journey across open waters. It becomes scary and unpleasant for all.

My friend Tim Smith helped sail an 80-foot yacht on a 1,200-mile journey from the Virgin Islands to North Carolina. Just before they sailed, the crew of 10 sailors was reduced to just 5 hearty souls. In retrospect, the captain was overly optimistic. The weather report called for smooth sailing, but we all know how reliable weather reports are.

At first, the trip was absolutely blissful. Tim saw seagulls riding on the back of a sea turtle on the open waters. Whales came right up to the side of the yacht in a friendly manner. It was magical and mystical. But it wasn't long before the five absent crew members were sorely missed.

Reports of fair weather turned out to be less than accurate. Storms moved in and sea swells kicked up. Soon the crew encountered the Gulf Stream current, which flows north as they headed west. Within a couple of days, they went from balmy, idyllic seas into full-fledged, batten-down-the-hatches storm conditions.

The group was stretched to the max in good weather but quickly discovered they were absolutely outmanned and overwhelmed in fierce conditions. They were no longer having fun in the least. My friend wondered openly if he was ever going to see his wife and children again. After a number of days of delay and battling the high seas, the yacht crew finally made port, but not until they had all gained a few more gray hairs and a firm determination to never board an undermanned boat again.

Struggling churches may seem just different at first, even a little adventurous. An element of excitement comes in starting something new and striking out with a pioneering work. And, indeed, there is something incredibly exciting about pioneering something from scratch. The problem becomes immense, however, when that pioneer phase seems to endure for the long haul of a church's life.

To start something up is an introductory scenario, not the long-haul behavior one can expect to walk out over years and years of church experience. For those in the struggling church, this rut-like experience week after week, month after month and year after year of not making progress becomes an expected way of life. One's entire Christian life can become a burden if progress is not made in the arena of church development. I am here to tell you it is not normal to experience that level of hardship forever. This should only be a passage we experience on our way forward toward growth and progress. If we are not making progress, we are likely making some fundamenta¹ mistakes in our leadership or vision. There are untold options of leadership missteps that could be at fault, but I am here to tell you that perpetual pain is not the will of the Lord for you and your people.

2. The "Visionless" Church

At times the difficulty that keeps a struggling church continuing to struggle is a shortage of vision. Things have been down for so long that it is difficult to begin to dream of anything other than depression. It is difficult to begin to think outside the box, which keeps the entire system and all of its contents shaken down. What can a person do to escape this negative, horrible treatment of his soul? The best thing is to simply escape by all means possible and necessary through the opportunity of vision. At one time or another, all of us have had an ample supply of vision. The difficulty comes when we have gotten off track with the degree of vision we had or currently possess. Being vision poor is a passing condition. Vision poverty can be overcome without a tremendous amount of difficulty. How do we grow larger than our lack of vision? We must allow our hearts to expand significantly in the presence of what we see coming for the organization.

Now is the time to get on board with the vision that God is handing out. He is the one who is in the business of handing out vision from on high. God is the provider of all vision. It's that simple. It is a matter of keeping our eyes squarely focused on who God is, first of all, and then what He's up to above and beyond that: who He is and what He is up to. He is an acting, thinking, doing God. He is active in human history and He is active in our lives today. There's no getting around the fact that God is at the center of the acts of His activity, His church, His Spirit as much as He ever has been in the history of the Church.

3. The Ego-Driven Church

This church is the worst of the mega-church world. Have you ever driven into a town and seen a billboard advertising a church—and most of the billboard is a photo of the pastor's face? Or maybe the church is large—even super-large—but refuses to multiply through local church planting? Have you been around a church that keeps adding onto its facility for no apparent reason? If so, perhaps you've been around the third type of unhealthy church structure, the ego-driven church. Here are some characteristics of this kind of church:

- It has no great or redemptive reason for the desire to grow large; it just wants to be large!
- It has over 1,000 members in weekend attendance (at least it acts as if it is very large).
- It is senior pastor oriented.
- It lacks clear identity. That is, every two to four years there is a shift in focus as a local church.

Such a church is an inwardly focused place. While there might be talk of outreach on a regular basis, there is actually little or no real outreach going on. Just as bad as the mega-church is the medium-sized church trying to appear larger than it is. The problem with both churches is that they don't know why they are trying to be large; they just really like being large.

A mega-church can be healthy if it is willing to give itself away. However, I've rarely seen an ego-driven church make the switch to a healthy church.

Some of these churches are going to extremes to not expand by multiplication. They are raising tremendous amounts of money to build amazing facilities that will allow upwards of 10,000 people to assemble at one time. My question is, what are those churches going to do when the magical, mystical senior leader passes from the scene? Make no mistake about it: he will pass from the scene, and in all likelihood that will happen sooner rather than later. In each case, the popularity of the senior pastor is what keeps the system going forward.

4. The Launching-Pad Church

The first sort of healthy structure is the launching-pad church. This is the best of what the mega-church has to offer: it regularly uses its largess to spawn new congregations. Here are some characteristics of a launching-pad church:

- It has a regular attendance of more than 1,000.
- It is ordained by God.
- It is financed by God in obvious ways.
- It has a deep bench depth (talent pool).

It consistently sees the birthing of new congregations as normal and reproduces itself in a variety of ways.

The prominent churches in the New Testament were all launching-pad churches. Today's launching-pad churches are often "teaching churches" offering internships throughout their structure. Staff members do not only do their jobs, but they also receive outsiders who are peering into their system and over their shoulders to learn how to effectively do ministry of a variety of sorts. These are "laboratory churches" that are continually trying new approaches to learning ministry.

One can't just go away for the weekend with local church leadership and decide to build a launching-pad church. It is up to God for these things to start. Of course there is a need for an openness and a willingness to be a part of something like this, but ultimately these amazing places are started by the will and the sponsorship of God Himself. God needs to call your church to be one of these churches. They require sovereign amounts of money, sovereign amounts of talent, sovereign amounts of vision and, above all, sovereign capacities to strategize how this will all be accomplished. All this will be supplied by God on a regular basis. The good news is that God is in the sponsorship business. He is keen on starting this kind of church.

The Great Church

There is a second church structure that is healthy, in addition to the launching-pad church; and this kind of church is the focus of this book. Just like in the children's story of Goldilocks finding the "just right" porridge, it's the church of 300 to 500 that's "just right" in most settings. Here is a summary glance of this church:

- It has an average total weekend attendance of 300 to 500.

- Its orientation is competence, not competition. It is the "good enough" church that would cause Maslow to rejoice, because it is filled with people who are transformed.
- It is large enough to be able to plant a new church now and then.
- It is large enough to be able to enjoy the strength of a varied staff.

During the last couple of decades, everything in the church has been subject to comparison. For a pastor, the question begins, "Are you like . . ." and concludes by naming the leader of a well-known church that has great visibility somewhere in the world. We've been steeped in the disciple-making church, the seeker-targeted church, the prophetic church, the power-of-the-Spirit church and the-gifts-of-the-Spirit church. We have been drowning in a sea of hyphens! The above list only names the hyphenated approaches I have been influenced by over the past decade and a half.

I have a simple thought; maybe it's too simple, but here it is. What if we gave up on the notion of living out the specialized church ideas from this point forward? From now on I refuse to put a hyphen in my descriptive name. I will no longer describe myself as anything-*sensitive* or anything-*driven*.

All of the well-known examples of these specialized churches can offer good testimonies. At the same time, none can be reproduced with any semblance of the success of the original because the key, it turns out, is the founder of the concept. The one-of-a-kind apostolic leader is the one and only person who can really work the idea the way it is supposed to be worked. I've read all the books by these one-of-a-kind leaders, and not one acknowledges this fact, but it remains a fact just the same.

I'm not looking for another (fill in the blank)-hyphenated church. Those journeys are for souls that are younger and less traveled then mine. If anything, I am seeking to build the generic church—you know, the one with barcodes on the front of it.

The older I get, the simpler I like things. Jesus said to love God with all our heart and soul and then love our neighbors as ourselves. In Jesus' words, we find a picture of a church operating at a practical level, without an agenda or program. We see a church that lives out the truth that it is better to give than to receive and better to love than to be loved.

I dream of a simple church marked by the simple proposition that we are "otherly." I have spent about 20 years operating on a belief that the only good and relevant church was the big church with a weekend attendance of more than 1,000—the kind of church that is among the largest in its city and on the road to becoming nationally known. When I came to Cincinnati, I set out to plant that sort of church. Deep in my heart, I felt that if my church and the other churches I started didn't grow to that size, they weren't really accomplishing what God sent us out to accomplish. It's funny how God tends to bless our faith. He did grow a number of very large churches in that city in due time, but that is not the end of the story.

Over the past few years, I've begun to seriously rethink that assumption. I've come to believe that, instead of having one church with 7,500 in attendance, which is the size of the Cincinnati church I started, what if we had 15 churches of 500 spread throughout the city? Or maybe even 20-plus churches of 300? This notion has utterly revamped my perspective.

Let me be clear: I'm not making an ideological statement with the term "pretty good church." Rather, I am contrasting "pretty good" with what I see is the predominating spirit of the Church age, which is marked by a penchant for extremes in excellence. The modern evangelical church—the seeker-sensitive church—seems to have come to the conclusion that if we are to do it, we need to do it more than just the right way—we need to do it with great excellence. I like the words of Christian thinker and writer G. K. Chesterton who lived around the time of World War I. Chesterton said, "Anything worth doing is worth doing poorly." When he spoke those words 100 years ago, he prophetically saw that we would struggle in our day, that we would be tempted to fall down at the feet of excellence and worship it instead of using it as a simple tool of perspective for ministry.

As we proceed through this book, we're going to begin with simplicity and focus on a total of 13 points to lead us to an understanding of the "great church." As I see it, the characteristics of the great church are described in these words:

1. Simple
2. Upward
3. Outward
4. Anointed
5. Fun!
6. Safe
7. Inclusive
8. Trusting
9. Atmospheric
10. Generous
11. True
12. Cooperative
13. Leading Out

Not one of those 13 characteristics emphasizes a numerically enhanced perspective as a priority! So let's begin first with a look at simplicity.

Notes

1. Alan J. Roxburgh, *Missionary Congregation, Leadership, and Liminality* (Harrisburg, PA: Trinity Press International, 1979), p. 20.

2. "Telephoning Churches Often Proves Fruitless," Barna Research Online (August 22, 2000), www.barna.org.

Chapter 1

SIMPLE
IS THE GOAL

A friend of mine was preaching in Kenya a couple of years ago. Part of his purpose in going to Kenya was to convey the essence of servant evangelism—that as you serve people with the kindness and generosity of Christ, they open up to the gospel. In one church of several hundred people, everyone became excited about showing God's love in practical ways. In fact, the people became downright stoked!

One Sunday, the pastor announced spontaneously that all were invited to gather the next Saturday morning at the church and go out to do a service project together. To everyone's surprise, nearly everyone in the church showed up! Armed with containers, the people locked arms to form a human daisy chain and went out into the community to pick up every speck of trash they could find. The pastor described them as a human vacuum cleaner. As they made their way through the city, you could actually see where the kingdom of light had come and where it had not yet appeared on the scene!

The cleanup crew's work stunned people around town that day. Everyone that the people from the church came in contact with asked about what they were doing. One of the curious was a writer for Kenya's national newspaper. She asked lots of questions along the lines of "Why in the world are you doing this?" When the people responded that they were doing just what Jesus would be doing if He were in Eldoret, Kenya, the writer said, "I always thought this is the sort of thing that Jesus would be doing if He came to town."

The writer was sufficiently impressed to write a great story about the outreach efforts, include a photo of the church people and place it on the front page of the weekend edition of the nationwide paper. This was the first time a positive article about any church had been posted in that national newspaper.

The beauty of that story isn't that people did something great in the kingdom of God and were recognized for it; in picking up trash, they did something very basic. What is significant is that they got excited about serving, went out and did a simple thing and affected their community immediately.

That's beautiful simplicity.

I wonder how many American congregations would respond similarly? How many church bodies would get that excited about doing something so practical? How many pastors would have the desire (or authority) to stand up and say, "Let's go for it this Saturday"? I suspect that in many cases a number of meetings would take place before something like this could happen. And when it finally did happen, it wouldn't be announced to the entire church; that would be too forward. A select few would be invited, and far fewer would attend.

> *Jesus was the simplest—and most effective—person ever.*

Jesus' purpose in life came down to one sentence: "By myself I can do nothing. . . . I seek not to please myself but him who sent me" (John 5:30). That was His guiding philosophy in life and the way He approached all of ministry. He uttered these words immediately after healing a man who had been lame all of his life. This man was just one of many in the crowd of perhaps a hundred or more. Jesus walked through the crowd, likely stepping past many who may have been equally disabled or ill, and went directly to just that one man. Jesus offered healing to that one man only. After seeing that solitary person healed, everyone was amazed, including the apostles. They were trying to make sense of this experience. Why had just one been healed? Weren't others worthy of healing? Why did this healing experience seem so fickle? The Pharisees were also upset—even though they had just seen Jesus heal a man lame from birth—because Jesus said He was equal with God.

Jesus didn't address any of the issues that were on people's minds. Instead He made this a matter of the heart. He put it all back to His relationship with the Father: "I judge only as I hear, and my judgment is just, for I seek not to please myself but him who sent me" (John 5:30).

The Challenge of Simplicity

When Jesus called people to repent and believe in Him, He used a phrase that, according to *The Challenge of Jesus* by N. T. Wright, was the dynamic equivalent of a modern command to "give up your own agenda and trust in me." We are called to abandon our little plans that are independent of the working and power of God and take up the plan of God in a big way. Apart from the plan and working of God, we are destined to failure. Mostly though, we are going to be abandoned to depression and isolation apart from getting involved in the plan of God, Big God, who calls us to join forces with Him. Our plans apart from His central involvement will amount to nothing more than self-sabotage. Yet with Him there is no telling how far and how wide things can go. His plans, with His empowering, can go the distance every time.[1] Jesus calls us, through His original band of believers, to an agenda of simplicity. To pull that off, we must trust Him deeply. So simple, and effective. Those two words—"simple" and "effective"—ought to always go together in the church world. Consider the simply effective life of the following two people.

Look-Alike or Live-Alike Guy?

Have you read about the guy they call What's-Your-Name? He's a man who sports long hair and a beard, dresses like one of the apostles and wanders the country doing small acts of kindness in the name of Christ. He owns nothing beyond what he wears. When people ask his name, he answers, "What's your name?"

"But has he been effective in his task?" you ask. People have reported physical healings (one man said that What's-Your-Name laid his hands on the man's ailing car and it started!). In Hazleton, Pennsylvania, his ministry to the teens caused many to give God a chance. He has prayed for people in the hospital who have been healed and released from their symptoms. Local clergy report that hundreds have returned to church as a direct result of the ministry of What's-Your-Name. If that's not simple effectiveness, it will do until the real thing comes along! He attempts to live his life in the presence of God continually.[2]

Way of Consideration

Another example of simple effectiveness is George Smith, head janitor for a suburban St. Louis high school. Just hours after buffing the gymnasium floor at Fern Ridge High School, he was standing on it in cap and gown. The 32 seniors of the graduating class chose George Smith as their commencement speaker. The seniors said they chose him not because of the job he does, but because of the man he is. One graduate said, "He's been so much more than just a janitor. He's helped, you know? He'll talk to you if you have a problem . . . and he's just a wonderful person."

The national news caught wind of George's story and asked him, "What's the largest group of people you've spoken to before this?"

His response: "I guess about four or five guys at a backyard barbecue or something."

"This is the greatest honor that I have received," Smith said. "And now, even at my favorite gas station . . . people are pointing and saying, 'Hey, that's the guy we seen on TV,' you know? So it's changed my life."[3]

Don't Walk

Kim Corbin is the head of a worldwide movement of skippers. It's not a fellowship of sea captains; skippers are people who skip wherever they go. They have discovered the joy and the many health benefits associated with the childhood practice of skipping.[4] Life can be defined in the simplest terms of success and failure when the parameters come down to "Are you skipping everywhere you go, or are you not skipping?" The skippers know that they are fulfilling their mission in life if they are skipping everywhere they go. If they merely walk or run or—heaven forbid—ride a bike, they are skipocrits!

In a similar way of dedication, there are the highly dedicated ones who live in the UK. Have you heard of the SoulSurvivor movement? In a country that isn't exactly known for its vibrant churches, this group gathers a couple of times a year to do just two things: worship and serve. By day they hit the streets in a variety of ways. They are especially fond of sprucing up dilapidated sections of town that need a good cleaning or a fresh coat of paint. Serving all day gives them an appetite for worship. They gather each evening for several hours of encountering God through intense and intimate worship.

Simple Discovery:
De-churched People Want Simplicity

The "de-churched" are those people who have given up on organized religion because it's too complicated, too irrelevant and, bottom line, not worth the time and effort of getting involved with. What they are looking for is what is understandable, simple and straightforward in the language of the common person.

The de-churched are more difficult to reach and communicate with than the merely "un-churched" of the 1980s and '90s. They are looking for authenticity, transparency and reality. They won't have it any other way. If you ask a de-churched person why he doesn't attend, he will likely tell you words to the effect, "It's just not worth it. It takes too much energy to get to a place that is too out of touch with life. Once I get there, I'm not edified. In fact, I'm bummed out. Then once I leave, it takes a couple of days to recover emotionally. Frankly, I have better things to do with my life."

Many of the de-churched are believers. They love the Lord; they just can't handle the complexity of the church as it has come to be in their minds.

Of those who don't attend church, only 2 percent stay away because they don't believe in God. The rest simply can't handle church for one reason or another.[5] This is a significant point to note. People don't have a God problem, but they do have a major church problem. Actually, the public can't handle church for a lot of reasons. For those who have ears to hear, the message is clear: People are looking for something more basic and straightforward.

Simple Discovery:
Sensing God's Presence Is Essential for Success

Much of what people are looking for in terms of experience in church can be easily summarized as the simple notion of God's presence. Once we have experienced a strong sense of God's presence, we have pretty much hit upon all the goals that we've been shooting for in terms of starting something that is fantastically winsome as a church. A church that regularly experiences the presence of God through its worship and in general when they come together and have a sense of the overriding conviction that God is among them—those people will have amazing things happen in their midst.

If we have a strong sense of God's presence, we have accomplished the mainstay of what we are shooting for in terms of success. There isn't a lot more that we can ask for if we have the assurance of God's presence. We are the ones who get to experience all that God has for us when we say we have tasted and seen that God is good.

Simple Discovery:
Clarity Is Essential for Success

I used to do a fair bit of target shooting at an indoor target range. I invested quite a bit of money in my equipment, to the point that I was equipped well enough to become pretty accurate. My level of accuracy took a couple of leaps up when I purchased a laser sight for one of my pistols. Once the pistol was "sighted in," hitting the center of the target was so accurate it was hardly even a sport. The bull's-eye, even at the end of the range, was easy to hit every time as long as the gun was even slightly steadied.

Every so often that same indoor range had what's called "Machine Gun Night." Machine gun owners in the area were invited to come out and shoot for free for the evening. The best part, for a target shooter, is that anyone who wants to shoot can also have a go at firing a real, live machine gun if he provides the ammunition.

The first time I fired a machine gun, I was completely unprepared for the experience. I had seen plenty of movies where the hero comes along and saves the day with machine guns blazing in both hands at the same time. In reality, a machine gun is just about impossible to keep steady. Machine guns are incredibly inaccurate and tend to move upward as they are fired. In my ignorance, I actually ended up blasting away at the ceiling most of the time!

The way that most leaders in the church approach leadership is more like wildly firing a machine gun than carefully aiming a laser-sighted weapon. Most churches don't know who they are, why they exist or where they are headed, and they don't have a clear idea about how they are going to get there. After asking, "Who are we?" an equally good question is, "Who aren't we?" Then, of course, there is the matter of trajectory; hence, the question "Where are we going?" These are all mystifying questions in many churches.

It is essential that we clarify our reason for being and our vision. If we hope to be effective, we must communicate these guiding factors and get the powers that be on board at the same time.

The words "church" and "complication" are too often synonymous. In my travels around the country, I am finding that new church plants are commonly being advised that, unless they have several hundred thousand dollars in hand, they dare not start their work. Too many leaders are frozen in their tracks, not knowing where to go in the current maze of complication the church finds itself in.

Drowning in a Sea of Complication

We need to take heed of the principle of Occam's Razor, put forward by the fourteenth-century logician and monk William of Ockham. Occam's Razor, also known as the law of economy or law or succinctness, states that to explain any phenomenon, one should not increase, beyond what is necessary, the number of entities required to explain anything; the greater the complexity of the system, the greater the need for simplicity.

We need to get rid of the extraneous and get back to basics. The most complex things humans have created have come from the most plenteous and simple things found in nature: sand, oxygen, water, fire. For example, the silicon chip that drives the brains of computers is made up of sand that has been fired.

Jesus, who lived on purpose and had a reason for doing everything He did, followed this simple and direct lesson. The more complex matters seemed to become, the more He sought to simplify what was going on around Him.

Simple Discovery:
The Straightforward Style to Services Is the Best Approach

How does the law of economy, or law of succinctness, relate to the way we compose the order of a church service? What is the most straightforward and direct path to accomplishing an effective corporate church gathering?

The 60-Minute-or-So Service

Over the years, I have experimented with church service lengths that varied from significantly less than an hour (far too rushed) to close to two hours (enough said—what was I thinking?)! I have come to the conclusion that approximately 60 minutes in length is just right for people in almost any culture. There are many who have grown accustomed to longer services than that, but that is a learned capacity.

There's something special about the length of an hour. There is something about that 60-minute period that seems to be hardwired into the human psyche. (That could be why the LensCrafters optical stores built their trademark on the promise to take care of people's optical needs "in about an hour.") The reality in our culture dictates (and in most cultures truth be told) that people can't endure more than one hour. We can pleasantly bear up with most things for about an hour, but much past that is challenging.

It was no mistake that Jesus chided the apostles, as we read in the account in Matthew 26:40, because they could not endure with Him for an hour as He prayed in the garden before His crucifixion. As humans, we are naturally organized into hour-long segments of time. The hour has been the natural measurement since the dawn of timekeeping when man was putting sticks in the ground and making crude sundials.

Not many churches really do substantive hour-long services, even among those that last 60 minutes. They try to cram too much in. It may be true that only 60 minutes elapsed, but an hour-long service was not accomplished. Church leaders often squeeze a 90-minute service into 60 minutes.

Some may feel that by limiting services to an hour we're accommodating the culture too much. Tension will always exist between what is culturally relevant and what is biblically counterculture.

The following components describe a church service that I see as the most important elements to ponder to accomplish a reasonable hour-long service.

Welcome

At VCC (Vineyard Community Church), we start by connecting with people early on and telling them what we're going to do while we're together. And we always start on time. We have a countdown on the video display that goes right up to the second of when we are starting so everyone knows when we will begin; the time is in huge digits in front of them. Someone with a cool demeanor comes out to say, "We're glad you've chosen to invest the next hour with us. Here's what we'll be doing. We'll sing a few songs with catchy choruses that are easy to learn. The words will be on the screen at the front if you aren't familiar with them. Then someone is going to tell you what's going on around here this week. Then we'll look at a video [or see a drama or hear from someone for a minute]. Finally, someone is going to talk from the Bible in a very practical way for 25 to 30 minutes. This will be the fastest hour of your week, and we believe the best-invested hour of your week. Let's worship God together!"

When we tell people what we're going to do, they can relax because they know exactly what's going to happen. What we do is much like what a host does at a fine restaurant. He makes people feel at home by telling them what to expect and what the specials of the house are.

PowerPoint slide between services:
"Please turn off cell phones and pagers
and set phasers to stun."

Worship

The worship portion should be about 22 minutes (see chapter 2). People in general are not able to enjoy more than that amount of music/worship. Only those highly acclimated to an atmosphere of worship can gain something great out of a longer worship set than that. (We at VCC occasionally offer longer worship settings, but usually not on Sunday mornings, and not without significant explanation and a heads-up before people arrive.)

Transition

When it comes time for announcements, use another word to describe them. The word "announcements" sounds parental and has a talking down quality. There are better terms to use that will help you build your own atmosphere and allow you to develop something unique to your setting.[6] And please don't refer to the newcomers as "visitors." If you aren't careful, the new people will begin to believe they really are visitors and will not return a second time. This transition time is your chance to talk to newcomers. Include them right from their first time among you by calling them newcomers. Assume that the newcomers are "one of us." In general, the way you treat newcomers will determine whether or not you move from the struggling mindset church to the Great Church.

Say for example, "If you are a first-time newcomer with us today, I hope you feel entirely at home. We would love to get your name just to know that you were among us today and to send you a little bit of information about us. We promise that we won't overwhelm you with information or bug you. No one will show up unannounced at your door. We promise!"

Note: *Never do anything to embarrass newcomers.* The only people new to a church who like to stand up are highly entrenched churched people. Anyone who is slightly introverted or uncomfortable or unsure of the entire experience not only will not stand up, but they will also make a careful note that this church is *not* a safe place. That newcomer will not return and will likely tell others who are willing to listen the same information.

As you make plugs (announcements) for upcoming events, remember that you're speaking to the entire congregation. Don't plug these events as if you're talking to a small family; and don't plug events that apply only to a small portion of the gathered church. Talking about these events in this way tells newcomers that we are oriented toward "us," not "you." To give that idea is to entirely miss the mark of communication. What you have to do in order to become effective is connect the dots on your way out of the debris field.

Take an offering. *One* offering. And don't make too much of a production of the offering. Newcomers and money do mix, but you have to be graceful when presenting the topic. General guidelines for connecting with newcomers on the subject of money:

- *Be mindful of how you talk about money.* It is fine to talk about money in a forthright fashion. You don't need to be reticent in your addressing money in the presence of newcomers. They can handle the topic. Just be mindful of how you talk about money. Churches can sometimes be overly sensitive to the topic of funding. They end up undercutting any talk about money for fear they might chase off newcomer traffic. The name of the game is to avoid making people feel guilty about money. Shame or guilt is a horrid way to handle people in the arena of the church on any topic, but especially anything related to funding.

- *Treat first-time people as newcomers, not visitors, from the beginning.* A newcomer will come back for the second time in a long line of routine weekends at your church as church involvement becomes part of his life. A visitor, well, visits once and that is enough.

- *Seek to assimilate newcomers right away* through heartfelt, intelligent interaction.

- *Don't embarrass newcomers.*

Video/Drama/Life Stories
An effective church service needs something to connect with the people between worship and the message. This can be either

a setup for the message or a standalone humor piece that adds to the total atmosphere. I'm big on building atmosphere, so I'm inclined to do humorous pieces most of the time.

You will have to choose between video and drama. For years we tried to use drama, to no avail. It nearly always turned out corny. Frankly, most of the drama I see in churches as I travel is every bit as corny and overdone as what we experienced. Each time I see a church drama, I think, *Now I remember why we stopped doing drama!*

I am biased toward the use of homegrown videos. Video does have its advantages over live performance. For example, it's precise—you know exactly what you are getting. Live performances vary in time and quality. Also, people are conditioned to watch a video. Video allows for a lot more creativity than live performance. Video can be done anywhere there's a screen and a projector, or even a television and VCR in smaller settings. And it can be done again and again.

Theology is easy; humor is difficult.
Dave Workman

Message

For the message portion of the service, 25 to 30 minutes is about as long as people can endure. I know from listening to the tapes of well-known pastors from around the country that it is common for weekend messages to run 45 minutes. It works for them, perhaps, but it isn't a good practice for someone who isn't an advanced or highly gifted speaker. As a rule of thumb, if you have just 20 minutes of message to give, then speak for 20 minutes. Limiting your speaking time requires significant self-control, but it's nothing you can't learn to do with a little practice.

Close

Give people an opportunity to respond to Christ. At the end of worship and a message, when people are gathered together, they are, by and large, prepared to briefly ponder the notion of following Christ. Sometimes this concept is abused by pastors when they prolong what some call the "altar call" and make it into something that God is not doing at the moment—thus placing pressure upon people when God is not putting that pressure upon the hearers. If you can learn to merely give people a simple opportunity to listen to the invitation of the Holy Spirit to come around to the opportunity of entering the Kingdom, you will be doing something wonderful for all of your hearers. You will be giving not-yet-believers a chance to come around. You will be equipping the already believers in the fine and simple art of how to connect their friends to the good news of Jesus. And it is indeed simple!

I do this connecting through a number of different ways. One is the "Look up if you'd like to make a faith commitment" approach. While everyone is listening with bowed head, I ask those who would like to respond to simply look up and meet my eyes to indicate they are in agreement that they desire to follow Christ. I clarify to them that this is for those who have never before understood or acted on the notion that God has personally invited them to follow Him. I put the pressure of the invitation upon God, not upon the cleverness of the invitation I am making. I tell people, "Somehow God has clarified to you that He is inviting you to follow Him. I don't know how He has done it, but you do. He has made it clear to you that He is making a personal invitation to you today. He is here in this room today, tapping you on the shoulder in some fashion. All that is important is that you are aware that He is making an invitation to you. By looking up, you are acknowledging that you realize He is inviting you to follow Him."

If people are holding hands during the prayer and response time, I ask them to squeeze the hands of the people on either side of them if they just responded to Christ. This approach is a great way to launch a discipleship relationship between the new follower and a more mature Christian. That older believer whose hand is squeezed will now become involved in inviting the new believer to a group or pray for them or perhaps just invite them out to lunch after the service. Of course it is easy to establish formalized follow-up programs for new believers, but those seem to not work as well as organic, natural means of connection that spring up spontaneously. I've tried both ways, and the spontaneous approaches tend to work a lot better.

It's no wonder we struggle with simplicity. We live in an anti-simple society and in a time of complexity. We have developed amazing numbers of choices. You can choose from 25 types of tissue for your nose, 750 kinds of cars and more than 43 kinds of Snapple tea.

Another approach is to simply close the service with a special prayer. I say, "Today, if God got your attention for the first time, and you are feeling as though God is inviting you to follow Him, you need to take note of that. He can get your attention in many ways—through the worship, through a prayer, through reading the Bible or through something that was said. If somehow God spoke to you for the first time, that's a signal that you need to respond to Him. Pray this with me; say this simple prayer as a way of presenting yourself to God: 'Well, God, here I am.' "

That prayer is probably the simplest and shortest prayer of repentance on record. It is the one I prayed many years ago in coming to Christ. It worked for me. I have prayed it with thousands since then, and it has been a good starting point for many who have gone on to do extremely well in their walk with Christ.

Simple Discovery:
Simplicity = Focus

One of the church planters I'm working with told me recently that he has three cards in his pocket, each labeled with something he's working on—outreach, celebrations, and small groups. He gave each of his leaders a recipe box with three index cards in it, and the cards were labeled with the same three priorities. I think he has the right idea. Working on just those priorities, he'll have his hands full for the next several years, perhaps for the next decade. What a contrast his approach is to the complex "we have to be good at a bunch of things" approach taken by so many new churches. If he succeeds in those three areas, he will have a great church.

Simple Discovery:
Simplifying = Saying No to Many Good Things

To simplify you have to choose to do some things and choose to not do some things that are currently on your plate. For most of us, choosing the top three priorities, and truly giving ourselves to those priorities, means we are going to have to *un-*choose about 67 other things on our plates.

For me it was my beloved Friday night seminars. I had conducted a series of equipping seminars on Friday nights for some time. They were fairly well attended. They made me feel good because I got lots of strokes when I did them. The people who attended them liked them. I taught for an hour on the gifts of the Spirit for example then concluded with a prayer time that was rather exciting. Each time I did it people told me I was gifted at both the speaking part of things and especially the prayer part. Plus those evenings were fun. I'm not sure where they fell when I numbered my priorities, but they weren't in the top three. When I became ruthless with my simplification agenda, the Friday seminars fell somewhere between priority number 4 and priority number 70, so they had to go.

Simple Discovery:
Simplifying = Pain

You have to get to the "I quit" stage before you can become truly simple. Getting simple is unbelievably painful and difficult. As I look back at my venture through leadership, I see many "I quit" episodes. At the time, they seemed simply painful, chaotic and meaningless. Now as I reflect back on them, I realize they were, in fact, times of greater simplification. I was becoming more effective at each turn in the road.

Simple Discovery:
The Most Important Word Connected with Simple Is *No*

You don't have the resources to do more than three things well, nor do you have the time, so you're going to have to be a person who has the courage to say no. You have to be the person who decides what the list of 3 is going to be. If you listen to all the people in your world telling you what the 3 things are, your list will be 173 items long.

Imagine you're growing a fruit tree. As you prune the tree properly, it will bear more fruit. If you look at churches that grow from 100 to 200, they became increasingly simple at every step along the way. They possess the ability to focus upon the things that are important, and they ignore the things that are of no importance.

My concern with the amazing number of church-building how-to books is that each offers such clearly defined answers in neat packages. The books allow little wiggle room for the reader, little room to deviate and listen to the Spirit. In their attempt to help others find the way forward, some authors have introduced another layer of complication. They have muddied the waters and made the difficult task of navigation even more difficult. We need to keep it supernaturally simple.

How to Move Your Group Toward Simplicity

- Shorten your services to 60 minutes.
- Treat newcomers right.
- Aspire to be simple and effective—God tends to provide us what we seek after all.
- Have plenty of signs to direct people.
- Carefully define yourself with your list of three things.

Notes

1. N. T. Wright, *The Challenge of Jesus* (Downers Grove, IL: InterVarsity Press, 1999), pp. 43-44.
2. "One Small Pennsylvania Town Taking Notice of Itinerant Preacher Who Calls Himself What's Your Name," *Good Morning America,* ABC News, February 16, 2000.
3. "Fern High School Janitor George Smith Gives School Their Commencement Speech," *Today Show,* NBC News, May 29, 2001.
4. You can check out their passionate love for skipping at their website—www. iskip.com.
5. George Barna, *Re-Churching the Unchurched* (Ventura, CA: Issachar Resources, 2000), p. 25.
6. I recommend using the term "plugs." The word "announcements" sounds like you are about to waste the time of everyone listening. As the camp song goes, "Announcements, announcements, announcements—what a terrible way to die . . ."

Chapter 2

OUR AIM
IS *UPWARD*

It was Sunday night. My wife and I had driven more than an hour to get to the crowded Southern California gymnasium. On the drive, I asked myself, more than once, why I was going so far, when I was already tired, to be part of something so out of the way like this. Even though we got there 10 minutes early, it was difficult to find a parking space. After the long trek into the building, the only seats my wife and I could find were the cheap ones where the temperature hovered in the upper nineties. The place smelled like sweat. It reminded me of a boys' PE class!

The worship leaders in this volunteer worship band were decent musicians but not spectacularly skilled. They were very casually dressed. Some wore shorts. Several dressed in beach clothes with no shoes.

The songs were easy to follow. There was something unique about them. For one thing, they were written in the first person, and they were directed to God. They weren't about God; they weren't directed to the people. They were all sung to God with lines such as, "We are here to worship and adore You." The songs were sung with passion and heartfelt fervor. The enthusiasm was contagious!

Soon I felt a spectacular and profound presence of God in the room. It was like nothing I had experienced before. People's reactions to God's presence varied: Some wept, others lifted their hands in the air, and still others sat in absolute silence, not wanting to disturb the manifest audience of God's Spirit.

Prior to that time I had only sung songs about God, songs around the atmosphere of God; but now it seemed as though I had broken through to the other side to experience God with a large group of people. The entire time was not the least sappy or directed from the front. Other than all of us singing the songs in unison, there was no human leadership to this time. There was a near spontaneity to this time. By the expressions on the faces and the conversation afterwards, I could tell I wasn't the only one who felt that way.

That was my first experience with transcendent worship— worship that goes beyond songs that are just well executed or diligently sung to a living interaction with the Holy Spirit. Transcendence is getting beyond singing songs to the place of encountering God through spiritual songs. This makes all the difference in the world when it comes to worship. Indeed, this is an authentic expression of worship.

Power Principle:
Change the Struggling-Church Mindset in Worship

No matter where your church stands in terms of momentum, it is possible to be ignited today by an adjustment to your worship. It is possible as well to have decent momentum happening throughout your entire system but lack forward drive in this essential area of your local church only to lose momentum throughout. Struggling in the area of worship is something no local church can afford. We must do what it takes to excel. But how does a local church do this well from the very beginning of its history?

Determine to/Avoid

Be great in worship. Avoid attempting to be excellent in worship. By being great, we are living up to the ideal that comes with loving God with heart, soul, strength and mind. We are wholly available to love and serve the God of heaven and earth. When we do things with enthusiasm, we are operating in the power of greatness. We cross over into attempting negative excellence when we try to do things in our own power. When we are operating in our own strength, no matter how excellent, we are no longer doing things that are worthwhile. The outcome is something that always looks like us in the end instead of something that looks like God. Excellence is a boomerang that is sent out from man and returns to man and looks like man at every turn. In contrast, true worship is that what we are up to looks increasingly like God, not man.

Lead people in worship. Avoid directing people in worship. As we lead people we are able to show people the way forward. As we model to others with our lives, we are showing them. The road that points toward momentum is paved with personal connectivity and modeling.

Show people a lot. Tell people little or nothing. In worship we can get to know the heart of people and they can get to know us as leaders. Without the willingness to become known, we are not going to get very far in leadership. This is more than a mere willingness—it is an enthusiasm for becoming known by others in this area of being known. As we are known, we are able to show others the way forward.

At the same time, we are not the ones who tell people much of anything. Our role is not to be tellers of things but to be showers. We point the way of God. We are the ones who go before others; we direct people forward; we point the way to the place where God is actively moving and alive in present tense. As He is moving in the current now, we are able to show the way to life.

Have a Success Mentality Going for You

It is absolutely essential to do worship well from the beginning of your church's existence. Worship is what people experience first when they come to your celebrations. It is the takeaway that people will hide in their hearts when they leave. When someone asks what they remember of your church, more likely than not newcomers will spontaneously express their take on what they sensed of God's presence that was or wasn't felt in worship through song. If you are the teacher, this may be difficult to hear, but it is the truth.

Newcomers will judge your church by your worship. Even those who don't participate in the worship will make judgments about the quality and philosophy of your church's ministry based on their first few minutes of interaction with you. If they like other aspects of your service but don't like this portion, it is not likely they will return. The reverse is true as well; if they like your worship well enough, they can overlook other aspects of your church that they aren't excited about, at least for now. They are likely to take on an attitude of, "Because we like the worship so much, we are patient with those other areas while they develop."

Here's a caution for smaller churches: You have to get past acting like a small family during worship. The natural tendency for less populated and sometimes struggling churches is to do what they think of as family-friendly worship. For example, children may be encouraged to be present with the adults during the singing portion of the service. I don't recommend this on several accounts. Little ones don't get much out of worship, in spite of what we adults would like to think. It just isn't fair to the children; they are bored being with the adults, and they are not learning to worship. At best, they are mimicking what they see big people do.

Some of that is fine, but some of it is going to come back later and bite children in the tail when they come into their own faith as teens. When these kids are searching for a faith to call their own, they need to have something to stand on that is significant, not a mimicked series of physical motions that were not meaningful in themselves. Children are often distracting to adults who are attempting to worship. Adult worship is often hindered while children are present. Children are nearly always far better off in another room with children their own age being led by caring, mature adults who are able to model worshipful experiences that are geared to that particular age group. If mom and dad want to do something further in the way of modeling spirituality at home, that is fine.

Overall, children will have a more positive experience at church if they spend the hour with other children. Let's spend our energy with children working on increasing the size of their hearts toward others instead of trying to do what is perhaps impossible in seeking to increase the probability of a worship experience with kids in their preteen years.

Power Principle:
Find "Big God's" Presence

It is essential that we encounter God—Big God's big presence—when we gather in worship.

I call it Big God's presence because that's what God's manifest life feels like when we are in the midst of it. I have felt the lack of God's presence in worship many times: "small God worship," if you will. I don't want to have a worship experience again without the full, manifest presence of God upon our time together.

Great worship isn't about doing brilliant things or finding astounding and highly gifted people to lead music ministry. Great worship is about simple yet profound God encounters. It begins with inviting the Holy Spirit to be upon our worship time and expressing to God our great desire to simply be with Him. Before this can happen, we need to identify the obstacles that prevent our experiencing God when we gather. A great worship encounter with Big God is never so much about doing everything right as it is about clearing the distractions from worship.

If you want to remove distractions, one simple rule of thumb is, to put it plainly, *Don't do goofy things during worship*. That is, clear the pathway of debris. It is the debris that prevents aircraft from coming in for a landing and causes difficulty in finding a place to light. In struggling churches, it often happens that someone suddenly feels led by God's Spirit to do silly things during worship. I have found that unplanned inspirations nearly always backfire and ostracize all of the levelheaded newcomers present.

"Let's All Come Forward"

For example, I recently watched as the worship leader of a struggling church acted on an uninspired idea. He said, "Isn't it great that we're all one extended family here? Let's all come up on the stage and stand here together and worship together." Everyone attending—about 120 people, including several newcomers—dutifully came up to the stage. Everyone was uncomfortable.

The worship leader later told me he felt momentarily inspired to do what he did but almost immediately regretted his actions. By the time he realized he had made a mistake in this directive, all the audience had already come up to the stage. The goofy idea ostracized all of the newcomers. (By the way, I disagree that a church is one big extended family. The use of such terms is a sure sign that a church is stuck in the struggling-church stage and it creates a negative effect on newcomers. They don't feel they are a part of the "family" and they don't get what everyone is apparently so excited about.)

One Song Too Many

An obstacle can be as simple as singing one song too many— singing five songs when four songs would have been just right. An obstacle might be the worship team gathering to pray in a huddle on the stage before a service. The huddle-prayer draws attention to the worship team members, making them look like they want to appear extra-spiritual. It's cheerleading from the front instead of leading the group into God's presence through worship. Prayer before worship is great, but the worship team should gather to pray behind closed doors.

We can analyze technical elements of the worship after the weekend celebration and plan to have skilled musicians galore for next week's celebration. But neither analysis nor plans will make a bit of difference if we don't profoundly and consistently meet God in worship when we gather.

Power Principle:
Avoid Complicated Worship

When you choose songs for your worship, check them against this list. Are they:

- catchy?
- memorable?
- simple enough to hear once and learn?
- enjoyable to sing?
- expressive of the heart of the church?

Consider writing your own songs if you have talented musicians. Homegrown songs can inspire powerful worship. Because the church is a living entity, it is natural that we will receive songs from the Spirit that reflect what God is doing in our lives. At some point early on, you need to decide if you are going to have piano-based or guitar-based worship. From my experience, it is easier to go with guitar-centered worship. The guitar is easy to follow. Ultimately, the question of guitar versus piano is a style question, but if talent is in limited supply, then guitar worship might be the way to go. There are many more adequate guitar worship leaders out there than piano worship leaders. Whichever type of instrumentation you choose, you can reduce complexity by keeping your worship set all in the same key or by singing several songs in the same key before changing to another key.

Guitar-based songs are more likely than not to have a rhythmic base to them instead of a melodic base. With rhythm, people can follow along easily.

Assembling a Band

If I were putting together a worship band, I would begin with a lead singer who plays guitar or piano and then add the following in this order:

Bass guitar: A bass guitar helps singers follow along. It doesn't draw a lot of attention to itself, so you might not realize how much it helps you. But when the bass is removed, it is difficult to sing along.

Second voice: If you have two singers, having one of each gender usually works best.

Electric guitar: An electric guitar adds fullness to your sound. Find someone who can play subtly. Overplaying the electric guitar distracts from the worship and draws attention to the guitar. This musician needs to blend in and play filler material, not lead licks.

Third voice: More voices add more depth to the vocal sound.

Keyboards: Keyboards, like the electric guitar, back up the lead instrument.

Drums and percussion: Drums can do a lot of good in the right hands, but they can be distracting in the wrong ones. Find someone who has a light touch.

Video Evaluation

Every so often, I have someone videotape our worship set, from the welcome to the ending prayer. Another camera captures the facial reactions of people in the congregation so we can see how engaged people are at various points of the service. Then I watch the video—as painful as that may be—with our worship leaders. We pause the tape frequently to pick up on the good points and to see how we could improve various aspects of the worship set. It's almost always a great learning time. I recommend you try it.

Another way to simplify is to keep the focus on the music. Talking between songs tends to get in the way of worship. Those who have come to worship have come to sing to God, not to hear quips or admonitions from a worship leader who is trying to cheer the crowd onward. I also include prayer in this moratorium. If you choose to include prayer, make it short and sweet (and scripted, if need be, to keep it on track).

I've found that the worship experience is usually more authentic if the worship leader plays an instrument. Otherwise the worship leader seems to be performing more than leading worship. When the worship leader plays an instrument, the entire equation changes.

Power Principle:
Avoid Letting Worship Run Too Long

For some people, worship is an acquired taste. It's like coffee: At first taste, it may not go down all that great, but the flavor has a way of growing on you. Some people can enjoy a lengthy worship time; but usually the uninitiated can't appreciate a long swig of the good stuff. I can worship for a couple of hours without growing weary, but I've had to work my way up to that level.

We were, at one time, a "high worship" church. That is, we would sing worship choruses for up to 45 minutes. However, the long worship time made our church "seeker hostile." Our attitude was, "If those new people can't handle the presence of God in large doses, well, that's *their* problem!" The long worship worked fine for us, but for those who hadn't developed a taste for worship, it was far too long.

As more and more newcomers found their way into our midst, I began to feel that we were overdoing our worship time—that perhaps we had created an insiders-only club. So I began to do some research. I stood off to the side of church sanctuaries across America and observed how long the worship endurance of congregations was. I found the same result in almost every congregation, regardless of denominational background, tradition or stated values. People are capable of being engaged in worship for a maximum of about 22 minutes. After 22 minutes, most worshipers' attention span drops significantly. Needless to say, we made a shift to a 22-minute worship set, though it caused some consternation for a time among people who love to worship. But now participation in worship is on a significantly higher level than it was before we shortened worship.

> **Our Hurry-Up World**
> We live in a hurry-up world. Columnist Dan Kadison noted that the producers of the 2001 Oscar awards show offered a large-screen, high-definition television to the winner with the shortest reception speech. Julia Roberts said "No, thanks" to the television offer; she said that, since she already had a nice television, she chose to talk for a while. Michael De Wit, winner of the Best Animated Short, spoke for only 15 seconds and won the television. Still, no one topped Alfred Hitchcock's classic "Thank you" at the 1967 award show.[1]

Power Principle:
Focus

Who are we singing to? What are we singing about?

People need a transition from the parking lot to the presence of God, from their living room into God's throne room. Worship can provide that transition if you start by singing songs *about* God and transition to songs *addressed* to God.

People come to worship because they want to experience God. Anything that doesn't help people feel God's presence is probably a distraction. I've seen many things distract from worship, such as worship dance, worship flag waving (one time, I nearly had my eye poked out), worship jumping and worship calisthenics. The activities were no doubt intended to help worship, but in the end they were clutter that got in the way of people seeing God more clearly.

At the same time, I think we need to be more expressive in worship, not less expressive. One woman I know lost interest in attending church as a young girl because, after she danced one morning in church, she was informed that church was no place for dancing. She said she wanted nothing to do with a God who would be offended by her worship dance.

Creative forms of expression are great as long as they are truly expressive of those worshiping. People doing their thing off to the side while the rest of the church serves as impassive observers can have a negative effect. Unless all the people are engaged, creative expressions can distract them from the centrality of worship.

We gather to have an experience with Big God. We gather together to transcend our week and experience a time of intimacy with God. That's the goal of all our worship experiences. The simpler the better. The less clutter the better.

As a rule of thumb, if something strikes you as distracting, it probably is. We ought to pay more attention to our hunches. If we did, we would stay out of the weeds more often. Doing what makes sense is always better than doing what is mystical, no matter how spiritual it may seem on the surface.

Power Principle:
Worship Opens the Door to Evangelism

Are you aware of the intricate connection between worship and evangelism? There is great power in worship. Without the significant touch of God's Spirit in worship, evangelism in a celebration service probably won't succeed. I have experienced this time and again. When I pray with people making a faith commitment to Christ during a service, I make direct reference to worship as the sign that God is real and calling them to follow. At the end of a service, I will pray in response to the message, then I will say, "Some of you felt God's presence for the first time today. It likely happened as we were singing the worship songs earlier. If somehow God got your attention, if somehow He reached out and touched your life, make note of that right now. If that happened to you, that was God's way of prompting you to follow Him." Then I lead them in a prayer to begin to follow Christ.

Something special happens in us at the emotional and visceral level when we pour out our hearts in worship to God. When not-yet-Christian people are in the room with already-Christian people, even the non-Christians are touched by the overflow of that atmosphere. They are drawn to Christ.

> ### Breadth Versus Depth
> Although about 82 percent of Americans say they want to "experience spiritual growth, they lack the spiritual practices and disciplines that will take them there," according to the *Arizona Republic* newspaper, which quoted *Surveying the Religious Landscape*, a recent book by pollster George Gallup Jr. and consultant D. Michael Lindsay. "Spirituality in America may be three thousand miles wide, but it remains only three inches deep," wrote Gallup, whose institute has surveyed Americans' religious beliefs and practices for 60 years.[2]

Power Principle:
Your Worship Style Is Not the
Key to Your Success

Your church will be identified by your style of worship. People say, "Oh, you're the rock-and-roll church" or, "You're the contemporary church" or, "You're the acoustic-sounding church." You may even hear "Your worship sounds like the Dave Mathews Band." (Some people may take offense if their worship is compared to a secular band, but such comparisons are inevitable and, deep down, complimentary.)

At first glance, your worship style may seem to be the key to your success. After all, it's *your* sound. It's what people in your city associate with your church. You are highly invested in that sound.

In reality, great churches across America have sounds and styles that are very different from yours. Some churches are growing like weeds with a sound that couldn't be any more counter to your contemporary sound. I visited a church that claimed to hold contemporary worship, but people were singing Bill Gaither songs from 35 years ago.

I like those songs just fine, but they are not contemporary worship songs. Granted, compared to hymns from the Reformation, they are renewal songs and are contemporary. That church in Southern California is growing nicely. It is a Great Church. The people know who they are, and they are being who they are enthusiastically.

Utlimately, your style isn't what causes God's presence to come into your midst. In fact, style is almost irrelevant. God comes into your midst because hearts are hungry for the presence of God.

> ## Contemporary Worship Appeals to New Members
>
> "Protestant groups that have emphasized contemporary worship and electronic musical instruments, rather than traditional forms, show a dramatic increase in their appeal to new members," according to the Hartford Institute for Religion Research at the Hartford Seminary in Connecticut. However, the transition to contemporary music can be a struggle. The institute conducted a sweeping study of 41 religious denominations and faith groups and presented the results in Faith Communities Today.[3]

Power Principle:
Don't Be Completely Original

As someone once said, "There once was a man who said, 'I will be original or nothing.' In the end he became both."

There are lots of great models for worship out there. To get your worship going, find one and copy it. Consider setting up your band the way your model does it. Choose the same songs if you like the sound. If you like the way the guitars sound, strive for that same sound.

Don't feel bad about copying someone else's worship style. If the truth be told, the worship group you're copying probably wasn't original to begin with either. Most likely, that group adopted a number of styles over a period of time and the conglomeration of those styles is what you see in front of you. There's nothing new under the sun. You don't have to write your own songs. You don't even have to have your own style. Done correctly, the song "Jesus Loves Me" works wonderfully!

On the other hand . . .

Power Principle:
Don't Blindly Copy Someone Else

While choosing a pattern to follow is helpful in the beginning, eventually a church's worship will need to become its own. A church needs to connect to its city in its own language and use a metaphor that makes sense in its setting.

I've seen seeker-targeted churches imitate worship they've seen—complete with choreographed movements and headset microphones—only to end up with what I call Up With People worship.[4] They're imitating in a not-so-effective way something they've seen at a big conference. It doesn't work, and it's not worshipful.

Don't be afraid to be different, but be aware that people will grow weary of too much experimentation. Your church will eventually find its own sound, style and focus. Find it and be that.

Power Principle:
Do a Quality Job, but Don't Obsess About It

Nothing will kill the spirit of worship in your church faster than an obsessive and perfectionist worship leader who is so detail-oriented that he or she can only see the "mistakes" being made during the worship time and misses what God is doing in the service.

Once a service has started, it's time to get out of the way and enjoy God. There's little that can be done to change things at that point, except to make note of what goes wrong and plan to fix it by next week.

How to Become More Upward-Focused

• *Pay attention to flow.* Be aware of flow from one song to the next. Sing several songs in the same key before transitioning to another key. The same rule holds true for tempo and pitch. It's fine to vary the tempo, but going back and forth too much confuses people and disturbs an atmosphere of worship. I like to start out with an upbeat song that is about God rather than directed to God. We use this first song as something of a call to worship—to get everyone on the same page in worship. Then we transition into slower songs that are directed to God. We typically finish a worship set with another worship song that is upbeat and declarative—that is, more about God. We have tasted and seen that the Lord is good, so we sing about that.

• *Be deliberate in your song choices.* Choose songs written in keys that everyone can sing. Some choruses and hymns are written in such high keys that they are very difficult, for men in particular, to sing. It's no wonder men often complain that they don't like to sing at church. They get a sore throat from trying to sing songs in unrealistic keys! Before you decide to include a song in your stable of songs, you might test it by asking some men to sing it.

• *Keep things moving.* Dead space between songs is not good. Transitions between upbeat songs and quiet songs can be difficult. Filling that space appropriately can be uncomfortable, but it is necessary.

- *Grow your worship.* The more you grow, the less room there is for mistakes. What is forgivable when you have 100 people might stand out as a glaring mistake when you have 300. It is imperative that you grow the worship as the church grows numerically.

- *Have musicians play within their skill levels.* If your musicians are proficient in only three chords, then stay within that realm. Be aware that the more instruments you add, the more skill the leader and other players will need.

- *Know who's leading.* Don't enlist a worship leader unless you know that the person will be good at the job. A great worship leader should have humility, skill and a philosophy of ministry that's in sync with the direction of the church.

- *Choose musicians carefully.* Avoid husband-and-wife combinations in the band; if you have difficulties with one, you've lost the other as well.

- *Be aware of your musician pool.* When a musician starts attending your church, pay attention to that person. You will have to draw on your pool from time to time.

- *Promote from within.* Homegrown worship leaders are usually the best leaders. Finding a worship leader in your congregation can be a lot easier than hiring from outside. However, homegrown worship leaders take longer to train.

- *Keep musical skill in focus.* The ideal worship leader is a skilled musician who has been taught to worship, not the reverse.

- *Make everyone feel included.* Struggling churches have exclusive worship—more like the worship that takes place in a small group. Perfectly Imperfect Churches have inclusive worship—worship that allows everyone to feel at home.

- *Start small.* Having worship led by one decent guitarist with a decent voice is better than trying to create a slick, pop-band appearance. Authenticity is far better than slick professionalism.

The goal of worship must be that everyone become aware of the manifest presence of God in their midst. There's a time to prepare diligently, and there's a time to let things flow and enjoy the presence of God.

Notes

1. Dan Kadison, "Hey, Wait a Minute, Who the Heck Won That TV?" *The New York Post*, March 27, 2001, p. 7.
2. Kelly Ettenborough, "Where Has God Gone?" *The Arizona Republic*, February 25, 2001, p. J1.
3. "Faith Communities Today," Hartford Institute for Religion Research, Hartford Seminary. See http://www.fact.hartsem.edu.
4. "Up With People" was a musical group that toured the country during the protest era of the 1960s and '70s. The group tried to be uplifting with a message of "positivity," but most people found the group about as authentic as The Brady Bunch at a Jimi Hendrix concert.

Chapter 3

LET'S GO
OUTWARD

Betsy and Sally don't look wild and crazy, but they are revolutionaries. They are moms who are out to change the world! One Saturday not long ago, they were out with a band of servant evangelists on a unique mission: They were going door to door giving away toilet paper! As people came to their doors, the team said, "Hi! We're giving away free toilet paper to show Jesus' love in a practical way."

Most people would smile and say, "Thanks. We already have plenty."

Then the servant evangelists responded, "Yes, but this is Christian toilet paper! We're giving it in the name of Christ."

We make our outreaches engaging and as humorous as possible. Then they offer to pray for anything that is going on in the people's lives. It is common to have people caught a bit off guard and end up sharing things that are going on in their lives.

At one door, a woman accepted the toilet paper but said she didn't want prayer. She laughed a little at the notion that this was Christian paper. As they stepped away, she said to them, "Wait a minute. Are you the kind of Christians that believe in prayer? I guess I could use some after all." They assured her they were the kind of believers who prayed. The woman immediately burst into tears. "I have to talk to someone. I recently had an abortion. I now feel it was a mistake, but I can't believe God would forgive me for this." She was sobbing so deeply that she couldn't speak clearly.

Betsy and Sally prayed for the peace of God to come upon this woman. They prayed for forgiveness. They unrolled some of the toilet paper and used it to dab her eyes. As the weeping subsided, they were able to console her a bit.

"You know, you really need to come and hang out with us at church. You'd really like it. It's laid back. The messages are practical. The music is good. The coffee is hot. We think it would change your life," Betsy said.

"Oh, I couldn't come," she responded. "My kids are out of control. They aren't 'church-broken.' "

"That's okay," Betsy said. "They sound a lot like my kids. You bring them and meet me by the door." The next day the woman came with a couple of her kids. She did enjoy herself. The rest is history, as they say. Now that woman has been coming to church steadily since the weekend she met Betsy and Sally.

It really is true—many people are thinking of coming to church, but a small, even itsy-bitsy thing is keeping them from attending. By encountering some of God's people in the right context, all of the barriers are removed, and voilà—they are there!

Up or Out?

I don't know which comes first—looking upward or looking outward. Sometimes having a dynamic worship experience makes us fall more deeply in love with Christ, which causes us to reach out to the not-yet-believers God wants to include in His family. But sometimes it's looking outward first that leads us to worship—as we love the lost, we feel a need to worship God.

Worship and evangelism are knit together at the core. Both are on the same nerve path that conducts feelings to the deepest recesses of the heart.

People are afraid to be outward; the "E word" scares them. What images come to your mind when you think of evangelism? The church that seeks to become great will need to address this issue.

Christ Calls Us to a Revolution

To address evangelism properly, a little bit of change here and a little bit of change there won't do. We need a full-scale revolution. And every good revolution needs a good focusing statement. In radical circles, that statement is called a manifesto. Here's our manifesto:

"We exist to love our city into relationship with Christ."

It's just 10 words.

The leaders of nearly every church say they want to reach out, but it is difficult to know where to start once that idea is agreed upon. The Great Church is committed to doing basic, low-risk, yet effective ways of reaching out that just about anyone in the congregation can do and will want to do.

A good manifesto needs practical handles people can grab on to. Consider the following guidelines for outreach that will help you build a good to great church. As you take notes on your budding manifesto, why not assemble your own idea of what yours will look like based on some of these ideas.

1. Outwardness Comes in a Lot of Packages

Servant evangelism (doing acts of kindness and generosity to show people the love of Christ), caring for the poor and planting new churches constitute the language of outreach that I speak fluently. Outreach is like a tool belt full of gear. Being effective means learning how to use a variety of tools and having the wisdom to pull out the right tool at the right time to meet the outward need at hand. The key to making evangelism work is being faithful to carry out a decent approach that matches the need for the long run.

> **"I'm So Glad You Asked"**
> Singapore is a "fine city" as the saying goes over there. That is, there are hefty fines for dozens of things we see as acceptable in the U.S. and elsewhere on the globe. Fines are levied for infractions such as chewing gum or sharing your faith with someone of a different belief system. However, if someone asks about your faith, you are free to answer his or her questions. Believers in this small, multicultural city-country are increasingly using servant evangelism to get around this problem of sharing their faith. When they serve others with an act of kindness and generosity, such as something simple like giving away a bottle of water, Christians can say, "I'm showing God's love in a practical way." Naturally, Hindus, Muslims and Buddhists ask, "So why are you being so nice to me?" To that the Christian can say, "I'm glad you asked . . ." A conversation follows and the fun begins.

2. All Evangelism Is Good Evangelism

All evangelism is good evangelism . . . as long as it's respectful of the individual. Any sort of evangelism can abuse people and therefore be less than positive.

I am partial to servant evangelism, and I do that very well (what's not to do well—it's based upon simple manners for the most part), but I also enjoy knocking on doors now and then and using more direct approaches to sharing the good news of Christ with people. The point here: Regardless of the approach, you can "love" people into relationship with Christ.

Muscular Christianity

"The Bible teaches its followers to turn the other cheek. Then again, its authors had never heard of the Christian Wrestling Federation (CWF), where the meek are blessed with bone-rattling body slams and headfirst flips through the ring ropes.

"Don't look for 'Stone Cold' Steve Austin or The Rock on this circuit. Instead . . . CWF brings its fans Apocalypse, Angel, the Beast and Jesus Freak. It also brings something else—a message of faith and hope." This Texas-based group of about a dozen wrestlers is touring the state with a program that includes a series of matches followed by the gospel message. A CWF founder explained that the group cares about ministry first. Wrestling is simply a way to reach teens.[1]

---

3. Leading Others to Christ Isn't that Complicated

When I first received Christ, I did so pretty much on my own, alone and quietly. No one had ever explained to me how this process was supposed to take place. My homespun prayer was similar to what the Bible tells us the prophets said when they encountered God's presence. I prayed simply, "Well, God, here

I am." It was a prayer of deep surrender, and it was wonderfully effective at introducing me to the person of Christ.

A few weeks later, I explained to some other Christians how I had come to know Christ. They were aghast that I had not put my faith in Christ in the prescribed manner—the official "way that everyone receives Christ," as my friends said.

Lately, however, I've been rethinking the way we introduce people to Christ. I'm moving from a "Tell 'em how it is" to a "Let's discover salvation together" mode.

I want people to get past the idea that they understand Christianity because they went to Sunday School. You have to learn how to do it. You have to undergo an apprenticeship. Nobody really wants to love their neighbor as themselves.[2]

Stanley Hauerwas,
Professor of Divinity and Law at Duke University

How to Nudge Someone to Christ

I allow myself to be a witness-in-progress.

I describe myself as someone who is still discovering salvation. Even though I've clearly come to know Christ already, it's important that I not come across as being in the company of the arrived.

I was on a plane recently, writing on my laptop. That computer was colorful, and the lady sitting next to me commented

on that. We began to chat. She asked what I wrote about, and
I said simply, "People."

She said, "Well, it looks like you write about God. You
aren't a Christian, are you?" She asked with a sense of dread in
her tone.

"Yes, but not the kind you are thinking of. You see, I've
been a Christian for 25 years, but I'm still not very good at it.
I'm still practicing quite a bit."

She shared that she had been disappointed in life by a lot
of ideas she laid at the feet of God—that is, she blamed God
for various things that had happened in life and she couldn't
figure out how else to configure things. She saw God as the
fall guy for much that had happened in her decades of living.

After we had talked for quite a while about what it means
to practice a life of following Christ—that He is pleased with
our willingness to follow Him with a good effort—she admitted that she was attracted to the image of Christ that I clarified to her.

Eventually, she said, "This sort of Jesus I could get into—
the kind that lets you practice. You know, if we were flying to
Hawaii instead of Seattle, I think I might be persuaded to become one of you."

I also help people present themselves to God.

Most people are intimidated by the idea of praying with
someone to express faith in Christ. In some faith traditions,
making a faith commitment is not emphasized. Language
aside, many adults—even in church circles—have not clarified
their relationship with Christ. They might have a childlike
faith in God in general but not have a specific, spelled-out relationship with Jesus Christ. The physical, emotional or psy-

chological needs of those we encounter are important, but the experience of clarifying one's relationship with Christ meets a need in a class all by itself! Knowing that you are going to heaven radically changes your entire outlook on life.

Recently, a significant survey at VCC gathered data on the topic of evangelism, and I discovered several encouraging truths. First, I found that about 60 percent of the people surveyed are excited about sharing their faith. Second, most of the people surveyed (75 percent) have shared their faith on a regular basis (three to four times in the past six months).

The attendees of VCC are average people. While the percentage of people who share their faith may be higher than might be normal in other churches, I suspect that Christians would like to see this degree of evangelism in every church. The survey also found that, even when so many people are sharing their faith, people feel they are being held back from sharing their faith by a fear of rejection and a lack of training.

With these things in mind, here are a few principles I keep in mind as I try to lead others to Christ.

Keep It Loving

Don't be pushy. Approaching someone with a message of love and an aggressive attitude doesn't make sense. Unfortunately, this combination is found too often in evangelism.

Keep It Real

When you introduce Christ to spiritual explorers, guide them first to a place of discovery. Then direct them in a simple prayer of presentation—"*Well, God, here I am . . .*" You may want to pray more extensively with them later.

Keep It Straight

When sharing my faith, I first say that God can forgive and change me. I keep the focus on my weakness and stay far from the brokenness of others. Spiritual explorers are sensitive to anything that suggests an accusation or spiritual one-upmanship. Here's the message:

- God is for you.
- God forgives you and me.
- God can change you and me.

Keep It Simple

Remember—the main thing is to keep the main thing the main thing. I'm all for training, as long as it's reasonable. You can find many programs designed to help Christians share their faith. Just be careful not to make it too complicated or too lengthy.

Define *Normal* as It Applies to Outreach

If we don't specify what the desired norm looks like, we will forever operate in a hit-or-miss mode. In my interaction with churches, I have asked if going out into the community once per month to do outreach is reasonable. Consistently, I hear that it is. So we might say that normal outreach is monthly.

However you define "normal," your leaders must act according to that definition. Ultimately, the members of your church will only do what your leaders *do*, not what they *say*. Therefore, it is vital that the leaders of your church, especially the senior leader, buy into outreach as an ongoing value. If the senior leader is going out once per month with the membership, word will spread that it is normal to do outreach in this church.

Another aspect of outreach normalcy is financing. If outreach is truly a value in your church, it needs to be supported by budgeted money. Inadequate financial backing is common when a church starts outreach in a serious way. If you are jumping into evangelism in a big way—especially into servant evangelism, which can be a bit pricey—it is okay at first to seek financing from individual benefactors, such as businessmen in the church. Ultimately the church needs to get behind the efforts of the outreach activities.

Ask small groups to do an outreach every fourth to sixth time they meet. Encourage the groups to establish a regular outreach schedule so that outreach becomes part of the small-group culture.

Defining Outreach as Normal and Fun
The North American Mission Board of the Southern Baptist Convention sponsors summer Epic Adventures, which are servant evangelism outreaches to major cities across the United States. Epic Adventures, which is promoted as a "nonthreatening but high-impact" way to share Jesus, is getting a healthy number of takers to sign up![3]

Be Consistent in Your Outreaches
Do your "rounds." Just as a doctor sees his patients regularly, you need to decide what your territory is and get around in that area on a regular basis—even if going out means that you and your spouse go by yourselves to hand out bottles of water to

show Christ's love. The battle will be won by those who are most consistent. The difference between growing and static movement always comes down to consistency.

Tell Encouraging Stories Often

You'll build credibility each time you tell others in your church about an outreach experience. If possible, relate an outreach story at each service or at least once per month. If you have video capabilities, tape your outreaches and show footage with some musical background.

A Bicycle, a Broom and a Bible

Romain Joyce ministers from a bicycle to people from all walks of life. According to an article in the *Charlotte Observer*, the 60-something preacher has ridden through the streets of Mount Airy, North Carolina, since 1996, balancing a broom and a Bible on his Fury Spectra 10-speed. He rides where Jesus tells him to, he said, and cleans sidewalks as well as people's hearts, he hopes. Joyce keeps a note pad with him to record prayer requests. Mostly people want to talk about marriage problems or addiction, he said. Sweeping and ministering full-time has always been a dream, he said. "The first time I did it, I found out God had a lot of hard work for me to do. I do the ministry every day when I can."[4]

Find Creative Ways to Make Outreach Prominent

Offer your church lots of opportunities for outreach involvement. Set up a table near the exit and supply it with outreach materials. For example, set out squeegees and window cleaner so that people can take the supplies with them to do their own outreach that week. Or provide bottles of water that people can give away as they hand out connection cards. Supply them with supplies the following week when they return—more connect cards, more cleaning liquid, more bottles of water, and so on.

While you are at it, collect great stories that are happening as people return from being out in the community. Give them cards on which to write their most recent stories and set up a box into which they can drop the cards. Down the road you will be glad you collected the stories when you go to share them with newcomers who need to be encouraged to participate in the new ministry of servant evangelism.

Stay Involved in Social Outreach

According to Scripture, caring for the needy isn't optional. God has given us a heart for the "least of these" so that we will reach out to them in increasingly creative ways. It is important that we consider ministry to the needy as a normal part of the budget so that it continues as an ongoing ministry. It is not necessarily expensive to involve yourself in social outreach. It is something that takes a bit of focus and commitment on the part of the local church. When you are involved in the lives of the hurting in your community in big ways, God will show up in your midst in His personal big way that is nearly measurable. He is in love with the down-and-out. When we loan ourselves, our time and our finances to those who are in desperate straits, we are loaning ourselves to the Lord. We are always involving ourselves in a good deal as far as the spiritual equation of things goes.

> ### Outreach and Growth
> Half of this country's religious congregations are grow-
> ing and thriving, especially those that embrace social
> outreach, according to Associated Press writer Verena
> Dobnik's article about the comprehensive study com-
> pleted by The Hartford Institute for Religion Research
> at Hartford Seminary in Connecticut. According to the
> study of 14,301 houses of worship in 41 faith groups, a
> primary factor contributing to growth was social min-
> istries that reach out to the poor. Most congregations
> offer a food pantry; more than one in three offer tutor-
> ing youth; and two in three sponsor a thrift shop.[5]

"Tangibilify" the Gospel of Christ

If "tangibilify" were a word, it would be a great one. It means
we need to make God's Word real by walking it out in genuine
ways. We must be a humble people who are self-deprecating
and don't take ourselves too seriously. We must be the kind of
people in the pew that people in the streets can relate to. Great
churches have a "whatever it takes" attitude. That's what we
are doing when we make Christ tangible with every aspect of
our lives.

Create an Outreach Identity

What's your outreach identity? It's your number-one attractor
as a church. It's your primary credibility gainer in your city.
Your outreach identity is more important than your worship
identity. My primary approach to servant evangelism is cleaning toilets at gas stations and restaurants. I know others who

Outward University Students

As a junior at Trinity College in Hartford, Connecticut, Carrie Haslett spent spring break in a beach resort in Fort Lauderdale, Florida. "We lived on the beach, drinking banana daiquiris the whole day," she recalled.

The next year, as a senior, Ms. Haslett returned to Fort Lauderdale. This time she stayed in a musty cabin cramped with bunk beds and rose with the sun to hammer shingles onto a roof that will soon shelter a low-income family she has never met.

"This feels so good—to see the fruits of your labor so immediately is so gratifying," she said. "People here care more about doing something meaningful than they care about . . . how good their tan is."

Carrie Haslett was one of 67 students recruited by Habitat for Humanity's collegiate challenge. Other organizations also offer "alternative spring break" opportunities. Recently, some 30,000 students traveled to locales exotic and mundane, tutoring children, landscaping parks, building wheelchair ramps, cooking for the homeless and people with AIDS, settling refugees, leading rallies against gang violence, painting murals on inner-city buildings.[6]

rake leaves. Others give away sodas to show Christ's love. What do you do? You can have more than one simple approach to sharing the love of Christ. But in the end you must convey the love of Christ in an active way that is going to connect with people in profound and moving ways.

Make a Strong and Enduring Commitment to Outreach

In the ebb and flow of the Body of Christ, it is easy to get caught up in smallness of mind and thought. Life happens, people talk and occasionally there is controversy. Unless we are busy doing the outward will of God, we will inevitably fall prey to smallness of heart. We will get caught up in controversy and speculation about other parts of the Church, and, in general, activities that are not redemptive and are an utter waste of Kingdom resources. Living out a life of commitment to outreach keeps us from much harm to ourselves and others. Ultimately, we are doing ourselves a favor when we get involved in outreach. We are insuring the probability that we won't become absorbed in human smallness that is guaranteed to be something we will become caught up in otherwise.

How to Become More Outward

- Give people lots of chances to respond to the message of Christ in public settings. The more opportunities you provide, the more people will respond.

- Talk about and live out the value of outreach. If I were planting a church, I would have bottles of water by the door during the summer so that people could take the water with them to distribute in the community. I'd have rakes by the door in the fall.

- Even small churches need to talk about starting new churches. But don't try to do it until you have at least 300 gathered who are coming on an average basis at the home church and you are showing strong signs of growth. (To attempt another church launch when you are not yet stable enough to give away that well-intentioned group of people is going to come back and bite you in the tail sooner than later. It would be best to wait until you are ready to plant and can do it out of a move of good momentum.)

Notes

1. Selwyn Crawford, "The Bible Belts: Christian Wrestling Makes Clean Break," *The Dallas Morning News*, May 12, 2000.
2. "Amen Corner: News and Notes," *Atlanta Journal and Constitution*, August 18, 2001, p. 2B.
3. Their website is www.epicnow.org, or call 1-800-264-5129.
4. Sherry Wilson, "With a Broom and a Bible, He Ministers," *Winston-Salem Journal*.
5. Verena Dobnik, "Study: Religious Congregations Rise," AP Online, March 13, 2001.
6. Jodi Wilgoren, "Helping Hands at Spring Break," *New York Times*, March 22, 2001.

Chapter 4

WE ARE
APPOINTED
AND
ANOINTED

Two women sitting next to me on the airplane were curious about the people sitting around us who were excitedly talking about, of all things, going to the city dumps in Mexico City.

"Pardon me for asking, but I must have misheard," said one of the women. "I could have sworn that I heard some of your party say that you're going to the city dumps. That's not right, is it?"

"Why, yes," I answered. "People from our church come down once a month to attend to the needs of people who live at the city dump down here."

"Why in the world would you do that?"

"We just think this is the sort of thing Jesus does these days as He is walking around in the world today."

The two women explained that they were not churchgoers at all. They were part of an international dance group that was gathering in Mexico City for a few days.

One of them said, "It's like you guys are doing the same work Jesus did, only in more places than He did it."

By the time we got off the plane, the women were so excited about what we were doing that they were ready to help support our efforts financially.

Imagine that! People who had no interest in attending church, at their own description, were spontaneously interested in giving to what we were doing with the projects at the dumps in Mexico City. Further, they were asking if it would be possible if they could tag along with us to be a part of the projects we were going to be doing over the next few days. These women could see something that excited them. They could see the hand of God at work in ways that drew them in. It isn't that He is not at work in less compelling activities that are more mundane around church circles; but even a person who is far away from the connectivity of the Kingdom can see the compelling nature of such acts as feeding those in need and providing medical care at city dumps.

Getting It Slowly

When I first came to town, I drove around the city with an aching heart—aching to connect with at least some of the nearly 2 million people in the city in a significant way. It was incredibly difficult to meet people in a strange city. The way I started up shop was completely organic—that is, I depended upon the natural networks of relationships and connections made from those from the beginning of things. This made for stable growth. We didn't spend any money on anything fancy in terms of advertising, but it was painfully slow at first, and I was the primary growth engine—my ability to go out and meet people was our entire growth strategy until we had a "snowball" built that was moving downhill fast enough that it could gather momentum on its own accord. The people I initially gathered were not well connected within the city. Because those we attracted initially didn't have extensive community connections to draw from, I had to start from scratch to develop a vision for beginning a church.

I began to take note of the deeds of the kingdom of God as they are explained in the New Testament, particularly in the life and ministry of Jesus. Where those deeds are done, the kingdom of God comes. It took me awhile, but I began to see that the kingdom of God isn't a time or a place, but an atmosphere that comes upon us when we do the deeds of the Kingdom.

One of the first things we did as a beginning church was to feed the hungry and "bring Christmas" to a group of needy families in a crack neighborhood. About half of our little church—12 in all—came together on Christmas Eve to give away food, Christmas gifts and Christmas trees.

The temperature that night was well below zero. It was so cold that we could feel the blast of cold air attacking our lungs as we merely opened the door to go outdoors. This coldest of days that winter, we saw children running around without coats and with shoes that showed bare skin through gaping holes. We stood in freezing homes to pray for entire families, sometimes with the gas stove burners blazing at full flame as people attempted to heat their homes. We prayed with children and with wives whose husbands were in jail. Some people told us that we were the answer to prayer; they'd been praying that their kids would have a Christmas. Some pointed us to other families who were in greater need than they were. Our hearts were filled with love for these families.

I discovered an important lesson: It is always better to be profound than to be clever.

During the next few weeks, people asked what was new at our church. It was natural for us to report what we had been doing. A businessman heard about what we were doing and was moved to give significantly to our outreach. More importantly, he began to talk to others about our efforts. For years after that, I heard from people that he had told about our outreach.

For years we tried using cleverness to start this church, but the results were minimal. No one listened to us. Then we started doing small, profound things—the simple things that Jesus did— and everything changed. Everyone was telling our story, and many were listening.

We have been at it steadily since then, and God has blessed our efforts. We have developed about 300 serving projects that get people into the community. Through these projects, we are serving hundreds of thousands of people each year in practical ways, as well as touching the community of the needy. Now, after 20-plus years in the city, we are known as the people who do acts of kindness and generosity. If you ask anyone in Cincinnati about the Vineyard Community Church, he or she will say, "They're the people who do the kindness stuff!" That's the sort of reputation you want to develop in your community.

Building Anointing

Your church's having a positive perception in your community is more powerful than words, programs, slogans and all the great sermons in the world. There is a big difference between cute and clever, and profound. To promote your church through conventional advertising is to be cute. Recently, I saw a church sign that read, "C-H-C-H—What's Missing? U-R." Groaners like this abound in the church world, and they don't bring people in. To get the word out about your church through anointed actions is to be profound.

What do people in your community think of your church? How can you turn their perception into something positive, even powerful? Jesus gave the answer when He said that the mark of a true believer would be simple acts of generosity (see Matt. 25:34-46). We want the city to describe us by the simply profound things we *do*, not by our cute slogans, where we meet or the charismatic leader we have.

Goofy Church Signs

Mary Katherine and David Compton collected clever invitations and admonitions they saw on church signs across the country and published their findings in a book titled *Forbidden Fruit Creates Many Jams*. Here is a sample.

God answers knee-mail

See U in S NDAY SCHOOL

Members Only: Trespassers Will Be Baptized

We aren't Dairy Queen, but our Sundays are great!

April First: National Atheist's Day

Free Trip to Heaven—Details Inside!

Where will you be spending eternity: Smoking or Nonsmoking?[1]

Building Block:
Be Anointed

What does the word "anointed" mean? Sometimes people associate that word with something vertical—something that only God can provide mystically to certain highly spiritual individuals. On the other hand, there is a horizontal aspect to being anointed and it has to do with the way the church is perceived by the watching world.

I have traveled around the world doing servant evangelism projects to demonstrate the kindness of Christ to people in practical ways. Because of these projects, I have heard the following words repeated hundreds of times in many languages: "I always thought that if Jesus were to come to us He would do things like this . . ." I've heard that thought expressed in Taiwan, Norway, the Netherlands, Germany, Mexico, Singapore and Russia.

Anointing is both vertical and horizontal. It comes from God, but people recognize it and are drawn to us because of it. It is our secret weapon when we are building the Perfectly Imperfect Church. Anointed behavior is fun. It's natural. You don't have to write up a business plan to practice anointed behavior.

Building Block:
Be Committed to Small Things

Mother Teresa said she did small things with great love. I've come to believe that is the best we can do.

> *Small things done with great love*
> *will change the world.*

When our actions are anointed, we gain credibility and people listen to us. All we can do in this life is small things; at least we can do them with great love. When we try to do big things for God, we often end up doing them with small amounts of love. More often than not, we make those attempts at great things out of our own strength, not from God's anointing.

Mother Teresa carried some 30,000 people from the streets of Calcutta into her small hospice so they could die with dignity. When asked what she learned in that time, the good mother squinted her eyes and said, "I learned that I wouldn't have carried the thirty-thousandth person if I hadn't carried the first person into the hospice."

Mother Teresa gained the attention of literally the entire world—one small step at a time. It's all about putting one foot in front of the other. It's about faithfully getting up one more day, even when we don't feel like it, and going for it one more time.

Building Block:
Be Real

People who are genuine in their behavior draw others to themselves. We need to be real. And we need tools for being real. For me the tool of choice is a toilet bowl brush. I regularly go to gas stations and restaurants and clean the restrooms to show Christ's love in a practical way. I approach the managers of the establishments and give them a big surprise by saying, "Hi, I'm here to clean your toilet." As they recover from the shock, I tell them this is a simple and very practical way to show them the love of Christ. This is what authenticity feels like for me. Commit yourself to some authentic behavior for a while.

I also try to pray specifically to prevent my prayers from becoming inauthentic and mystical. (As an exercise in authenticity, I recommend you read *The Velveteen Rabbit* by Margery Williams aloud every night for two weeks. It will do something great to your heart.) By doing a specific outreach yourself—one you don't share with anyone else—you force yourself to be in the "authentic zone." The whole "Christian zone" insulates us from authenticity. For a wake-up call, spend part of a day at your local Alcoholics Anonymous center. Don't spend all your time exclusively with believers. That gets weird.

Building Block:
Be Willing to Do What Others Will Recognize as Practical

One Sunday, as a friend of mine was enjoying a meal at a restaurant, he asked the waitress if she liked working on Sundays. She said she hated it because church people came in on Sundays. She said they are *hard* to serve, *arrogant* and *lousy* tippers. Her rule of thumb is that the longer they pray the less they tip!

Since that day, my friend has been on a one-man crusade to turn things around among his Christian friends. He asks them, "What if Christians were *easy* to serve, *really friendly,* and always *big* tippers?!" He now leaves a healthy 20-percent tip and writes on the bottom of his credit-card receipts, "Great job! I really appreciated your service today." He reports that almost always the server will come back to the table and thank him for his nice tip and the word of encouragement. His parting wisdom: "If Christians are going to act in an unanointed way, at least they shouldn't pray before they eat to draw attention to themselves!"

Building Block:
Be Willing to Take a Risk

Sometimes you have to step out and take a chance that you might look silly or even stupid. That's okay—it's worth it. Jesus was "anointable" because He was always willing to do the Father's will.

One year, when Christmas Eve landed on a Sunday night, we decided to cut our services short and do an outreach to the community by giving away donuts to policemen, firemen and others who had to work that night. The group I was with went to fast-food drive-thru restaurants. At each one, we pulled up to the speaker to order and heard the restaurant worker's voice ask, "May I help you?"

Then I would say, "No, actually you can't. We're not here to get food. We're here to give food."

"Sir, may I help you?"

"You see, we cut church short tonight so we could all go out and give away donuts to people who have to work on Christmas Eve. We're here to give you donuts to celebrate the evening."

"Sir, please pull forward."

At each restaurant, I pulled forward to find a number of employees huddled around the drive-thru window. In every case, the response was super positive; sometimes restaurant people had tears in their eyes as we drove away. The best response of the evening came at a Wendy's restaurant. After the workers cleared away and went back to work, the manager came to the window and said, "Thanks for making this an extra-special night."

"Yeah, this is a special night, being Christmas Eve and all," I said.

"No, not just that. My wife is having a baby tonight!"

"Then why are you here? Shouldn't you be with her?"

"Well, I'm pretty goal-oriented. I figured I could put in my shift here first and then meet her at the hospital. Besides, she's not that far along yet. One thing though—do you think you could pray for us tonight?"

I assured the manager that my son and I would immediately pray for him as we pulled away from the window.

I went through that drive-thru a few days later, this time with a baby gift. I signed the card, "The Donut Guy," and attached my business card. A week later, the manager came to our church with his wife and brought along a few friends—14 in all! I think he brought all of his in-laws and the UPS guy as well. He was downright enthusiastic about coming to church.

Building Block:
Be Committed to Producing Outwardly Focused Disciples

I'm convinced that the action that most pleases the heart of God is evangelism. Some might argue that discipleship should be emphasized over evangelism, but I disagree. Our churches must develop an outwardly focused people. Without a steady dose of evangelism, and without new folks coming to Christ, there will not be any new disciples to worry about. What could possibly please the heart of God more than finding lost children?

One day in heaven, we will rightly describe the church by its inward activities, but that day has not yet come. Until Jesus comes again, we must push ahead in the belief that the mission of the church is all about outwardness. As we are committed to loving others, the anointing of God will flow like a river in our midst.

Building Block:
Be Amazed When God's Anointing Appears

Surprising things happen when we live in the anointing of the Spirit. Outsiders recognize what we don't even see. For example, the SoulSurvivor young people's movement in England was recognized by the Manchester police. After the group's outreach there in the summer of 2000, when 1,100 young people did servant evangelism in the rough part of town, crime went down by 45 percent and has stayed down since that time.

Building Block:
Be Willing to Be Near the Least, the Lost and the Lonely

We have to spend time with the poor. When we are simply around the needy, genuinely looking for ways to show them God's love, God's Spirit flows through us.

Building Block:
Be Willing to Act in Simple Ways to Change Lives

For years, I read Matthew 25 with fear and trembling. I saw in it an awesome warning: You'd better watch out, you who think you are Christians. You might be a fake believer posing as a real one. You'll be exposed in the end. That warning is part of the chapter's message, but there is so much more.

One day as I was reading this chapter, I experienced a paradigm shift. Matthew 25 is actually a very practical chapter that gives the church its marching orders. Verses 34-46 provide our job description, not a haunting, frightening parable.

Jesus said, "I was thirsty and you gave me something to drink" (v. 35).

He was saying that authentic faith always acts. A real faith doesn't just say the right words; it does the right things.

Jesus said that we would prove the authenticity of our faith to the world by doing these acts of love. As we relieve parched throats by giving drinks of water and meet the needs of the hungry by filling their stomachs with food, the people of this world will know in their hearts that we are the real thing. There is no need to raise our voices and say more adamantly, "We are for real!" We simply require a few minutes of their time to show them the reality of our message. Our acts of reality speak for themselves. The history of Christianity is filled with this pattern. We move from claim to demonstration to assurance. All of it happens in a short sequence.

Building Block:
Be Willing to Get Away

The combination of serving and ministering can be exhausting. You have to be able to get away for renewal. It's easy in the midst of great things going on to get caught up in the adrenaline rush of the moment and forget to take care of yourself, but an imbalance between giving and renewing will not work for long. Anointing is great stuff, but we still need to tend to ourselves and the business of balance.

Note

1. Mary Katherine and David Compton, *Forbidden Fruit Creates Many Jams* (New York: New American Library, 2001).

Chapter 5

FUN!

Everything that could go wrong went way south that morning. It was Easter, which fell on the weekend that Daylight Saving Time began that year, and the janitor who was to open up the building slept in until the last minute. We got into the building just a few minutes before the first of our two services. By the time we managed to get things set up just 15 minutes late, everyone was stressed out. No one felt any emotional space for worshiping God.

All I could think of was Chevy Chase as Clark Griswold in National Lampoon's *Family Vacation* movie. "Are we having fun yet?" I asked. Everyone laughed and blew off some steam, and we were able to enjoy the Lord in worship.

Where the Spirit of the Lord is, there is fun!
2 Corinthians 3:17 (Almost)

A few years ago, our church made the national news when the so-called parking-meter granny was arrested in Cincinnati for putting a dime in a stranger's parking meter so he or she wouldn't get a ticket. The people of Vineyard Community Church had been feeding parking meters for years as an act of servant evangelism, completely unaware that it was technically against a city ordinance.

When the Parking-Meter Granny was arrested, we gained overnight prominence as the church that "illegally feeds parking meters to show God's love in a practical way." The situation got tense, to say the least. In Cincinnati it is considered bad manners to gain slightly negative national attention, so the pressure was on.

I decided to turn on the fun and flip the situation completely. First, I had T-shirts printed with a picture of our granny behind bars, and I had parking meters put on top of the bars. A caption read, "[name withheld], guilty of kindness." (I can't use the parking-meter granny's name in this book; she is currently in the Parking Meter Feeding Protection Program.) The T-shirts made a small statement about the whole event that was clever and slightly irreverent, and they quickly became collectors' items. The shirts were the talk of the town. In fact, they made their way onto several nationally televised talk shows.

We also made fun of ourselves in a video we produced. In the video, a guy is searching his pockets for coins to feed a parking meter. A policeman approaches in slow motion with ticket book in hand. Suddenly relief comes in the form of a "kindness helicopter" that drops off a quarter. The coin comes just in time, and the policeman (a real, uniformed policeman who is a friend of ours) puts his ticket book away. Both actors wave at the helicopter.[1]

We are all trying to do something significant to glorify God. It's only natural that we should think we must be serious about our task. But it's easy to be overly serious, and that attitude can work against our efforts. It's easy to be like a Norwegian pastor and friend of mine: "Ya, we Norwegians take our joy very seriously."

Unfortunately, we diligently remove any hint of enjoyment from our task when it's involved with the church. But that joyless attitude is not the heart of God, and it's not following the model Jesus gave us. In almost every other area of life, we know how to have fun, but in the church world we fall short.

After working with people in many different contexts for more than 20 years, I have come to the conclusion that people only do something for a prolonged period of time if it's fun. That is, they quit what is not fun. We are hardwired by God to do what is enjoyable.

Where the Spirit of the Lord is, there is fun! Fun is normal—that's a given in the Great Church. A playful attitude and a church culture that allows fun can cover a multitude of shortcomings in other areas. Because of grace, we can be just who we are, and just where we are in our progression of growth; who and where we are is just fine! The discovery of that truth is incredibly liberating, though not universally understood.

For many people, the first name that comes to mind when they think of a Christian (other than Jesus) is not the pope, Mother Teresa or Billy Graham. It's Ned Flanders, the goofy-looking, next-door neighbor on the television show *The Simpsons*. With his mustache, thick glasses, sweater and irrepressibly cheerful demeanor, he is the evangelical that non-evangelicals know most intimately.

An estimated 70 to 80 million evangelical Christians live in the United States, which means that one in every four Americans is an evangelical Christian. Although heterogeneous in their beliefs, politics and lifestyles, they recognize one another easily, and they would have no difficulty recognizing Ned and his family as their own.[2]

Ned is deeply committed to the good works of the gospel, including the random donation of a kidney and a lung to anyone who might need them. When a homeless man arrives at his front door, the family bathes him and treats his sores, gives him a new change of clothes and sends him on his way, singing "Onward Christian Soldiers" as they work. Ned is someone Jesus would have no trouble identifying as one of His own.

The only problem, and the reason he is the brunt of weekly jokes on *The Simpsons*, is that he doesn't have the first clue about how to have fun. The typecasting is faithful to the bitter end. Flanders is typical of modern evangelical Christians because we don't know much about fun either.

Are we having fun yet?

Clark Griswold,
in National Lampoon's *Family Vacation*

The Spirituality of Fun

Consider Bill, for example. A typical new church attendee, Bill faces some barriers when he decides to come to church. He hasn't been the same since his divorce, and he's still getting used to the idea of the kids being with him only every other weekend. However, he's heard from several friends about a certain church. (Plus people from the same church once gave him a soda as he waited at a stoplight.)

So one Sunday morning, he dutifully pulls on his only button-down dress shirt. It's a size too small in the neck, but he figures being uncomfortable is part of going to church. It's his weekend to have the kids, so he wrestles them into church mode. They aren't exactly excited about going. By the time he arrives at the parking lot, he's pretty nervous and not much in the mood to look for God, although that's what he came to do. Still he hopes for the best.

A couple of different things could happen when Bill arrives at church. He could have a negative experience. He could feel the same as my friend's child who reported after visiting a church one Sunday, "Dad, the pastor yelled at us for an hour!" Whether he actually yelled or not, it felt like he did, and that's all that counts. Many people no doubt feel yelled at even though voices are not necessarily raised. The attitude and context make them feel that way.

On the other hand, Bill could have an entirely different experience. Imagine how Bill would feel if he arrived on the church property and was greeted by a parking attendant waving one of those large foam pointing fingers you see at football games. Bill would probably smile and wonder, "What kind of church is this?" Imagine that attendants good-naturedly point Bill to a parking spot, and then offer him a cup of coffee right there in the parking lot. Imagine that they smile—a lot.

In this picture of Bill's church experience, he meets more smiling people at the entrance of the building. As he maneuvers his kids inside, someone sees his situation and directs him to the children's area. A uniformed policeman in the vicinity of the children's area helps Bill feel secure about leaving his children with people he has never met. As he moves toward the auditorium, he is greeted once again and handed a program that explains what will be going on during the service. Another smiling face directs him to a seat and answers his questions about this new place he has entered.

After worship, a video introduces the series the pastor is doing on "Facing Life's Worst-Case Scenarios." The video is over the edge, but Bill likes it a lot. Talking to the camera, the youth leader describes having "one of those days" when everything seems to be going wrong. In the background, his car starts to roll downhill, gradually picking up speed until it hurtles into a lake and disappears under the water.[3] Although Bill doesn't know the youth leader, he laughs until he's almost crying. The crowd is still laughing and clapping as the lights come up and the pastor comes out on stage saying, "All right! Let's continue in our series on 'Surviving Life's Worst-Case Scenarios.'"

Top Ten Ways to Know You're in a Bad Church:
(drum roll please . . .)

10. The church bus has gun racks.
9. On staff are a senior pastor, an associate pastor and a "socio-pastor."
8. The Bible is the Dr. Seuss Version.
7. There's an ATM in the lobby.
6. Services are B.Y.O.S. ("Bring Your Own Snake").
5. Choir members wear leather robes.
4. There's no cover charge, but communion is a two-drink minimum.
3. There's karaoke worship time.
2. Ushers ask if you want smoking or nonsmoking.

And the number 1 way to know you're in a bad church is that the only song the church organist knows is "Inna Gadda da Vida."[4]

Bill is all ears. His defenses are down. When the pastor asks people to refer to their outlines, Bill is happy to oblige. He's eager to learn. He's having fun!

Each time Bill laughs, his defenses drop a little further. He returns the next week and for the next couple of months until he eventually becomes a follower of Jesus.

Defining Fun

When I use the term "fun," I mean something different from what most Christians mean. It's not happy clappy. It's not fun as determined by children's church cutouts in Sunday School. It's not the "I've got the joy, joy, joy, joy down in my heart" fun. It's two parts the kind of fun you could have with your little brother when you were growing up and one part David Letterman. We discovered the kind of fun I'm referring to when Dave (my associate pastor at the time) became a bit irreverent.

It's fun for fun's sake. It's saying Christian people can be fun and a little silly. This kind of fun doesn't necessarily have much to do with the message; it's just plain fun. It doesn't have much to do with anything, but that's okay.

We must give people permission to not act "spiritual" all the time. People don't have to impress anyone to be a part of the church. They can just be themselves.

Vital Fun Fact:
It Is Important to Have People in Leadership with Whom You Can Have Fun

If you can be yourself and have fun with your team, your church will reflect that. If you can't, it won't. Talk with your leadership about the issue of fun. Discuss the way you want to relate to one another. You will likely have to start with small steps, but permission giving is a start.

Vital Fun Fact:
The Quality of Hospitality Plays a
Huge Role in the Fun Factor

Hospitality means a love of strangers. For example, it means making guests who have come by for dinner feel that you are thrilled they came to your home. Hospitality is what you want to convey when people stop by your church for the first time. It's the first thing newcomers will comment on when they mention your church. Because they will evaluate how friendly you are, make their evaluations work to your benefit.

Think about what it's like to go to your church. Then think about what it's like to go to your first ballgame. When you have no idea what the seating arrangement is like, an usher to help find your seat makes all the difference in the world. Having needs anticipated and taken care of is such a relief to a newcomer.

You might also think of newcomers as if they're guests visiting your home. What do you do when people come to your house? How do you make them feel welcome? You don't sit in the living room and yell out, "Come on in." You get up and greet them warmly. You invite them into an atmosphere you've tried to make pleasant by controlling the aromas and setting the lighting so that it's just right. You don't do these things to impress your guests; you do them because you want to bring your guests into your family, to include them and make them feel comfortable.

When we do servant evangelism projects to show God's love in practical ways, from washing cars for free or distributing soft drinks, to cleaning toilets, we are tacitly inviting people to church. We are saying, "God loves you," but we are also saying, "Now follow us to church." When we do that, it is our responsibility to make sure the newcomers' experience when they arrive is a positive one. In fact, their experience ought to be more than positive—it ought to be a party! My question is, "What do newcomers experience when they arrive at your church—a party or a funeral?" For the sake of our credibility, we need to have a fun environment waiting for them.

Vital Fun Fact:
An Atmosphere of Fun and Enjoyment
Creates a Reality Larger than Life

No explanation needed.

Vital Fun Fact:
The People Up Front Will Set
the Tone for the Service

If the worship leader, the transition person and the pastor/teacher are having fun, the people will have fun. On the other hand, people will quickly detect when a leader isn't having fun. It is imperative that all people up front have their hearts right before being "on" in public. Once these relationships are aligned, it is probable that you will not only enjoy your time together all the more, but you will also sense the flow of God's Spirit together. Don't forget, where the Spirit of the Lord is, there is fun. That fun is best experienced together.

Vital Fun Fact:
After Worship, the Fun Factor Is the Most Critical Component of a Service

What you set as the priority will become the priority, and almost nothing will change your church as much as building up the fun factor. The fun factor will permeate every aspect of your atmosphere—for the better! It's worth the effort to build enjoyment into your mix.

New people and veterans alike will comment on what they take away from your services in terms of what is memorable in this area of your services. It is a bit challenging to quantify all that comes together to make up an enjoyable time together. Such times are more easily recognized when they are not happening than when they are.

Vital Fun Fact:
Agree that It's Okay to Poke Fun at Each Other

The view of the pastor as "most highly exalted and most excellent" needs to be obliterated. This view advances the opposite of fun and is not worth propping up. It's also not an accurate view of any pastor. No person can live up to the stately notion of that kind of pastor.

Vital Fun Fact:
Humor Is Vital for Lowering People's Resistance

A friend of mine likes to say, "Theology is easy; comedy is hard." What makes people laugh—hence, what makes them drop their defenses—is what we are looking for. Remember Bill, the new-comer? Lowering his defenses each week made it possible for Bill to find his way to Christ. The fun factor played a large role in lowering those defense barriers a bit at a time. He came into a vital relationship with Christ and into a thorough relationship with VCC as his local church when he came to the understanding that church was a place where he could enjoy himself and get in touch with his brighter side—not a place that portrayed his stuffy and proper side.

Vital Fun Fact:
Dress Casually

Most people like to dress for comfort. Formal attire suggests formal, serious worship. If your church culture dictates formal attire, you're going to attract the already-believers who enjoy an hour of serious church. A formal atmosphere is antithetical to numerical and spiritual growth.

Frivolity

At least 1,400 college students are majoring in "golf" at eight universities, with more schools about to start such programs, according to an article by Toby Moore in *The Express*. One school just completed a million-dollar "learning laboratory" (a golf clubhouse). Across the country, golf courses are opening at a rate of about one a day.[5]

Comedy Void in the Church?

Hoping to fill the void, the *Los Angeles Times* printed what it called a new line of products for the Christian practical joker in its "Off-Kilter" column. Here's a sample:

- *Whoopee Pews:* $129.75. When unsuspecting parishioners take their seats at church, the whoopee pew emits noises better imagined than described!

- *Flaming Hot Communion Wafers:* $4.95. Slip some of these into the Communion plate and watch the fireworks. Looks like the real thing but makes eyes water and throat burn.

- *Throw-Your-Voice Talk With God Kit:* $74.99. Add life to your sermons! Increase collection revenues! Learn how to throw your voice into the choir loft, under the altar or into collection plates. Secrets of world-famous ventriloquists revealed in 32-page booklet. Kit also includes 50-foot-high, inflatable, glow-in-the-dark Jesus.

- *Leaky Communion Cup:* $14.99. Looks like an ordinary Communion chalice, but wine drips through tiny holes when the goblet is tipped. Especially funny when used with super-hot communion wafers.

- *Shock Hymnals:* $9.99. A victim who opens this book gets a powerful but harmless electrical shock. Never fails to catch the suckers when left around.

- *Flypaper Trick Bible (King James Version only):* $12.75. The Good Book you can't put down! Just like an ordinary Bible, but the pages are made from sticky flypaper.

- *Surface-to-Pulpit Projectiles* (set of six): $34.95. Pocket-sized projectiles that can be launched from anywhere in church with amazing accuracy. Keep those sermons short and to the point with these tear-gas bombs.[6]

How to Become a Fun Church

- Don't do church business on Sunday morning.
- Make sure everything is ready 30 minutes before the service so you can relax and have fun instead of feeling stressed because you are scrambling at the last minute.
- Consider using humorous video clips to augment your weekend celebrations. For a total investment of about $10,000, you can purchase a video projector, a great camera and an editing computer with software to get started in this ministry.[7]
- As a leadership group, have a heart-to-heart talk about having fun. Agree to enjoy one another. Agree to not take yourselves too seriously.
- If you are the pastor, decide to make preaching fun. Don't take yourself too seriously. Let God's joy flow through you. (If you prepare adequately during the week, you'll be much more likely to enjoy yourself when it comes time to speak.)
- Be yourself no matter what kind of personality style you are.
- Gear your humor to the crowd you have.
- Give yourself permission to have fun.

Notes

1. If you're curious, we still do servant evangelism to people in need of coins for their parking meters, but we no longer actually feed the meter. We attach the coin to the card and place the card on the car for the owner to use next time he or she needs a coin for the meter.
2. "How Many Evangelicals Are There?" Institute for the Study of American Evangelicals, 2005 data. http://isae.wheaton.edu/defining-evangelicalism/how-many-evangelicals-are-there/.

3. We didn't really roll the youth pastor's car into a river. We used a junker without an engine.

4. For this and other humorous "Top-Ten" lists used during weekend celebrations at Vineyard Community Church, check out cincyvineyard.com.

5. Toby Moore, "This Is America; Golf," Express Newspapers (April 13, 2001), p. 14.

6. Roy Rivenburg, "Off-Kilter: Churchgoers Don't Have a Prayer of Escaping These Practical Jokes," Los Angeles Times (March 17, 2000), E4.

7. If you would like to see videos we at Vineyard Community Church have done over the years, call 513.671.0422 and ask for VineBooks to order an assortment of these tapes.

Chapter 6

SAFE

After the JonBenet Ramsey murder, the

Columbine High School massacre and the 9/11 terrorist attacks, I don't have to tell you what kind of times we live in.

Question: If you were a pedophile, where would you go on Sundays?

Answer: Probably where lots of minimally supervised little kids are located.

We need to create a safe church environment at every level—physical, emotional and spiritual—if we hope to have a great church.

Safety is what people demand if they are going to bring their friends and family to our churches. Safety comes at many levels, starting with safe children's programs and safe facilities. Then there's the dimension of emotional safety that allows people to be real among friends and frees them to enter wholeheartedly into community. When these lower-level safety issues are met, people are able to be "in sync" with God. Once people feel a strong sense of safety with God, they are able to take risks and hear God's voice challenge them to step into new arenas of spiritual growth.

A major role of leadership is to create environments where people can feel safe as they take experimental steps forward with God.

So What's Safe Anyway?

Feeling "safe" is feeling the assurance that nothing is going to be forced upon a person at any time against his or her will or outside his or her comfort level. That feeling allows people to let down their guard, be themselves and engage in the activity at hand.

Safety was not what my church felt one Sunday evening awhile back. I'm fairly easy to distract when I'm speaking, but the circumstances of this service took the cake. Even the most focused speaker would have been distracted. As I spoke, I saw red and blue flashing lights through the windows at the back of the church auditorium. A few minutes later, I saw a couple of police officers haul a disturbed-looking lady in handcuffs by the back window. Of course, I wasn't the only one who noticed all this. Keep in mind that while all of this was going on, I was delivering a sermon! Later, I heard more of the story.

Earlier in the day, I had met a woman who told me that she was bipolar and had been off her medication for some days. Like many bipolar people who stop taking their medication, her claim was that she was feeling great, but the intensity she evidenced in conversations earlier made it clear that she was not doing well at all. I told her to go home, take her medicine and get some much-needed sleep. Instead of following my advice, she returned to our evening service. When our nursery number system called for a parent to tend to a child, she got the wild idea of claiming that child as her own. In her disturbed state, she went to the nursery, claimed to be the rightful mother and attempted to hoist the baby. Fortunately, we have a pretty decent security system for parents picking up their kids. When she couldn't produce her security pass, she tried to grab the baby and run down the hallway. One of the workers grabbed the baby, suspended her in a hold, then called the police, and she was arrested.

Probably the worst part of the incident was what happened in the news media. Her arrest was a matter of public record. It wasn't long until several television stations picked up on the story. In fact, it was going to be the lead story on one station's late news. We pleaded with the station and were able to convince them to put a positive spin on things. In the end, the story ran as, "Quick thinking nursery workers at local church avoid kidnapping catastrophe. Details at eleven." But the story could have had a far worse ending if we hadn't had a police officer on duty.

Over the years, we've been faced with many situations that challenged our church's safety zone, including people coming to church with lethal weapons, drunk people standing up during the message to comment on my talks, Pentecostal extremists shouting out in tongues (usually harshly), and people shouting angry prophecies directed at me as the pastor (some are funny even at the moment of their being spoken).[1]

The overall feeling is not so different from the tryouts of *American Idol* we have all seen on TV. Some think they can sing well, but when they do their thing in public, it comes out sideways. Each situation has to be handled quickly and appropriately to maintain the level of safety we want people to feel.

Physical Safety

Every parent who brings a child to church needs to feel fully assured that the child will receive first-class treatment and that there is absolutely no cause for any concern for the child's safety. To give families this kind of assurance, pay careful attention to details. You may find some of these statements worth adopting for your operation:

- We make sure that children are always with three adults; this is for the protection of both the child and the adults who could potentially be accused of something later.

- We don't allow men to care for small children under a given age.

- We do a background check on all children's workers to make sure they are "clean" from a police record standpoint.

We do a recommendation check as well on every single worker. Many people will pass a criminal background check but not pass a recommendation check from their previous church.

Sometimes we get information on people who have been in places of ministry with children or in other positions, and they need to be replaced while in an active role. It is necessary to talk straight with them and see them bumped out of a role, especially when they don't pass the recommendation check. I encourage you to take the time to do call-checking on people and see if they are for real or not. As difficult as it is to confront people in settings like this, you have to keep in mind the possibility that you may end up with someone in a ministry role who is not meant to be there, and the utter chaos just one such person can cause. You don't want to ever have to deal with anyone like this even once in a lifetime. It is always better to play it safe than sorry.

Physical safety also means designing the facility so that it promotes a sense of wellbeing. Our facilities have a window in every door. With the price of video monitor cameras increasingly affordable, it's feasible to put a camera in each children's room and have someone watch monitors in a central room. Videotapes/DVR provide a record that can be viewed later too. Bright lighting also gives a sense of security and safety. Children's facilities, in particular, should have bright lighting to reassure parents.

Safety and Comfort Zone

As a leader, you need to stay aware of and "jealously" guard the atmosphere of the church facilities. Are people sweltering because it's too hot? Make the building livable. Think of the five senses. How does the place smell? Professional cleanup and restoration companies can do wonders with a basement-type odor. Does the church look pleasant, or are the three folding card tables from three weeks ago still on the stage? Is the sound pleasing, or is it unbalanced? Take the time to analyze these details and make sure they are covered.

It is imperative that you inspire in parents a high level of confidence that the childcare is excellent. Have someone in a uniform around the children's area during services. That presence says: "I'm here to make sure the kids are safe. I'm not here because there is a problem, but because we don't want a problem." You can create a safe, fun environment for the kids while finding a balance between the need to have visible security and too many people walking around with badges.

No matter how good some men are with infant care, moms will more quickly allow other moms to care for their infants; so avoid having men and/or young teenagers be the caregivers for babies. Here are some other details regarding the security of the facilities: Provide lots of light; most churches could literally double the lighting to be where they need to be. Also consider how to provide open space and lots of glass to give yourself and others every opportunity to easily view what is going on at any time. And keep all secondary doors locked.

Put yourself in your newcomers' place. Imagine being at a Buddhist temple and not understanding much of anything that is going on, including the building. If you evaluate your facility from that perspective, you begin to get an accurate understanding of the way a newcomer views your place.

Too Safe?

The *Edmonton Journal* in Alberta, Canada, reported that specially commissioned Braille posters were displayed at two locations: the University of Alberta's human resources department and the Truro Leisure Center in Truro, England. The intent was to provide equal treatment for the blind. However, sighted people couldn't read the posters because the words were only in Braille, and the blind couldn't read the limited-edition posters because they were behind glass covers for "protection."[2]

Emotional Safety

Newcomers need to feel assured that no one is going to make them do anything they don't want to do. Allow newcomers to maintain anonymity for as long as they need that anonymity to feel comfortable. They also need to know they will never be embarrassed at church. Never!

Emotional Safety Zone

Pastors can enhance the feeling of emotional safety within a church service by disclosing their own weaknesses. Be real with people. At the same time, disclosures should be balanced by an ability to challenge people.

Here are some ways to encourage both regular church members and newcomers to feel more comfortable in church and become an active part of the fellowship.

Create an environment where all can focus on worship. Make sure one person's worship doesn't get in the way of other people's worship. I actually had to talk to some people who were wildly worshiping with sign language. People around them had cringed and ducked to avoid being hit by a flying gesture. (The worst part was that the sign-language worshipers were not hearing impaired.)

Interpret unusual events for congregants. At the beginning of one of our services, a man keeled over with a gallbladder attack. There was a scene, and paramedics were called. I conveyed/interpreted to the group that the man wasn't having a heart attack, that emergency personnel were on the way and we couldn't do anything to help this person other than what was going on. I suggested we ignore the emergency personnel as they did what they needed to do. That's what people did—they were able to ignore the paramedics because they were informed. We continued on with the service with amazingly few interruptions and closed out the service with little confusion.

Allow newcomers anonymity. Don't smother them; give them some space. Don't ever single them out. One of the worst things that routinely happens is the pointing out of newcomers in a large worship setting. Some mistakenly think that newcomers actually crave this attention. Not so. Also recognize that newcomers can be somewhat jaded. Avoid pushing them to give money. Pass offering bags rather than plates to provide a means for some anonymity.

Safe for Customers? I Don't Think So.

PrimeZone Media Network reported these findings about customer reactions to bad service:

- 39.3 percent complain to a store manager
- 25.7 percent tell friends about the experience and urge them not to shop there
- 22.2 percent stop shopping at that store
- 22 percent walk out without making a purchase
- 15.3 percent just ignore it
- 12.7 percent get upset but continue to shop at the store anyway[3]

Think about how these customer reactions might apply to your church.

Avoid insider lingo. Avoid referring to anything you would know but the person walking in off the street would not know. Don't say, "We're having the church picnic at Bill's farm again. It will be a great time, just like it was last year. Sally Smith will be making her good ol' apple pie once again. See you there." Talk as if you have a room of neophytes who have no inkling of what you are talking about. Provide the information people might need. "But there aren't that many newcomers yet," you protest. That may be, but there won't *be* many in the weeks to come if you continue to use insider lingo. Give newcomers a comfortable place to ask their questions. Give them permission to ask any questions they wish to ask.

Provide the right amount of follow-up after a newcomer's first visit. Avoid coming across as pushy. Pay attention to the wording of the letters or other types of communication you send to newcomers.

Spiritual Safety

An atmosphere of spiritual safety begins with authentic preaching. Authentic preaching means speaking what you've learned from your life's experiences and, often, from your own pain. Spiritual safety isn't something you institute late in the game; do it now. This basic understanding of how spiritual safety begins will positively color all of your relationships.

Spiritual Safety Zone

Allow people to pursue God at their own speed and at God's speed, not at your speed. We need to find new ways for people to pursue faith. Don't try to push anyone along the journey at a faster pace than he or she is prepared to go. There are two ways to get a chick out of an egg. One is the direct approach: Grab a hammer and use it on the egg. You'll get the chick out of the egg, but you will probably kill the chick in the process. The other approach is to put the egg in a warm, caring environment and allow the chick to come out on its own and in its own timing. The second approach is the way Jesus "incubates" new followers. He draws newbies along with warmth and empathy.

That is the way it works. And it's the approach that takes the power of love into account as its power for performance.

> ### How to Increase Safety and Comfort
> - Have every person representing the church wear a nametag.
> - Provide police protection in visible locales.
> - Develop a system for picking up children and teens.
> - Provide an abundance of signs.
> - Assume that you are dealing with unchurched strangers who have never been to your facility—and don't know where to go.
> - Include recommended area restaurants in your program. Chances are good that newcomers to your church are new to the area and don't yet know their way around.
> - Work on language. What do you call things? What do you call people? Do you insist that newcomers who join your church culture add your insiders-only vocabulary to their own?

Notes

1. My favorite "prophecy" was what I call the flying bologna prophecy. A disgruntled member said he saw me speaking with a winged hunk of bologna flying over my head. The word from God was, "Thus says the Lord, 'Steve is full of baloney!'" After he delivered that word from on High, he began to not attend church services. He felt he had "Made his witness" and he didn't need to come any longer.
2. *News of the Weird,* April 17, 2001, No. 688.
3. "Bad Service Drives Shoppers From Stores," PrimeZone Media Network (March 20, 2001).

Chapter 7

INCLUSIVE

The couple approached me with tears in their eyes.

"We've been in town for over a year, diligently checking out churches week after week. Honestly, this is the first one that has paid attention to us. We feel loved here. We were greeted four times before we made our way to our seats. Thanks for loving us."

By nature, churches move quickly into their own self-made universes. We all build exclusive cultures and keep out new people who are different. Newcomers can be changed by our message of great love, but unless the church makes an intelligent and heartfelt attempt to be inclusive, not-yet-believers will not meet Christ's life-changing acceptance.

If you are the senior leader, you are an ambassador to newcomers. Your job is to connect with as many newcomers as possible. There will always be hangers-on who want to dominate your time and who have a chronic problem that needs to be tended to. But the people you need to be meeting are the people who just got there, not those who constantly need prayer for something that doesn't exist. I pray briefly for people who are in need—one or two sentences is enough. My main objective is to mingle with newcomers or anyone I don't immediately recognize.

Acceptance Is Not Necessarily Approval

"Jesus, friend of sinners." That is a line from a hymn, and it about says it all regarding Christ. He spent His time with prostitutes, tax collectors and lepers; He would spend His time with the rejects of today given the opportunity. Who would He be with in today's world? He'd probably be with people who are confused about sexual issues.

Jesus accepted everyone on the spot, although He didn't necessarily approve of everyone's behavior. We must do no less.

People with certain issues are dilemmas for us, especially those who have crossed the line on issues of sex. The church doesn't know how to handle people who are attracted to people of the same sex or people who are sexually involved outside the marriage relationship. However, if we are determined to follow Jesus' example, we will reach out to people even when we can't approve of their behavior.

A few years ago, the Flynt brothers, Larry and Jimmy, came back to their hometown of Cincinnati to open a pornographic bookstore. Twenty years earlier, they had been booted out of town by the county sheriff. When the brothers became executives of the *Hustler* publishing empire, they desired a presence in Cincinnati. The brothers managed to maneuver around the local laws and finagle a bookstore, practically across from city hall, no less, to the embarrassment of many city officials. When the store opened, area Christians reacted. Many met the Flynts head-on with protests. One flyer I received urged decent Cincinnatians to picket the establishment until the Flynts were driven out of business and out of town.

My wife and I had a different plan. We decided to be more subversive. We packed up our toilet-cleaning gear and headed out for the first of what became regular visits to the Flynts' rest-room. We figured we'd show them the kindness of Christ in a profound way and invade their hearts.

The first time my wife and I went to the Flynts' store, we totally shocked Jimmy Flynt. He asked us to repeat ourselves a couple of times as though he must have misheard what we had said, but we repeated the offer. "Seriously, we just want to clean your restrooms to show you Christ's love in a practical way," we said. Finally, he silently pointed to the back of the store where the toilets were located.

About a year after we started the cleaning routine (the protests hadn't succeeded in closing the store), I found myself sitting behind Jimmy Flynt on a flight from Los Angeles to Cincinnati. I didn't automatically take my seating arrangement as an invitation to talk his ear off; so I waited to see if we would bump into each other. We did exactly that on our way off the plane. I said, "Mr. Flynt, I'm Steve Sjogren."

"I know who you are," he said. "You're from that toilet-cleaning church. The first time you came down to our place, I thought you were putting a bomb in our john!"

He continued, "What kind of Christians are you anyway?"

"We're the kind that doesn't hate you."

As we got off the plane, we agreed to have lunch. We haven't had lunch yet; I suspect he's a bit fearful. That would be natu-ral. I'm praying for an open door.

The distinction I make is between acceptance and approval. I was able to totally accept one of America's most notorious pornographers. I know he felt that acceptance, because he stopped dead in his tracks, even with people behind him trying to leave the plane, when I said we didn't hate him. I certainly don't approve of what he does. But if Jimmy can just give the Holy Spirit a chance to do some changing in his life, I know God will work out the details.

If we believe that God can work out the details in anyone's life, we're invited by Big God to embrace everyone who comes through our doors.

Follow Up on Newcomers

Our church may wait a long time before Jimmy Flynt pays us a visit, if ever. But he won't forget the church that cleaned the toilets in his adult bookstore, and God can use that kindness that so perplexed him to bring a spiritual influence on his heart.

In the meantime, we have a lot of other newcomers passing through our doors to welcome. Through years of experience, we have identified some effective ways to make them a part of our fellowship from the very first moments they meet us.

A Safe Request for Their Names at Weekend Celebrations

Many newcomers will be reluctant to give you their names or any other personal information during their first visit to your church. If they have visited churches before, they may expect to be hounded or called or spontaneously visited by someone from church. Any of those actions is absolutely unwanted by 99 percent of newcomers. No matter what they say at the moment, they are thinking deep down, "That's the last time I will be going to that church! It's completely unsafe."

I've heard of all sorts of approaches to making newcomers feel at home, from baking bread, pie or chocolate chip cookies to be delivered while still warm, to planting a sign in a newcomer's front yard that reads, "Thank you for visiting our church!" When I hear about such techniques, I always ask, "Is the church growing?" Almost always the answer is no. I believe that church leaders who checked would find out that all of those attempts to make newcomers feel welcome actually do quite the opposite to the majority of slightly savvy people. The direct shot right between the eyes is overkill.

Don't be dismayed when newcomers don't give you their names on their first visit. People are just that skeptical these days. I have found that it often takes three to five times at a church before people feel enough trust to provide an address and phone number. What I say to diffuse their fears is, "If you're new, we'd love to get your name and address. We promise that we won't bug you; we'll just send you enough information to answer a few questions you might have about this church. And we'll send you an ice-cream cone in the envelope!" (I'll explain that later. That offer intrigues them enough, most of the time, to give us their information.)

Some churches have found they're more successful at getting people to fill out information cards if they make the cards playful. One church used a cartoon drawing of a man; it looked like a card with legs and arms and with a bit of a worried face. The card read:

Please fill this out and circle the responses that are mostly true:

❑ I am here for the first time today.
❑ I've been here before, and I think it's an okay place.
❑ I'm getting hungry!
❑ I'd like someone from the church to call me about
   _____.

❐ I'm wondering when this service is going to finish so I can get home!

At the bottom were spaces for the newcomer's name, phone number and address. That card brought a very high response rate from folks. New folks enjoyed filling out the cards.

The Big Kahuna Principle

In our day, people are proud of their ability to make decisions and control their lives. Each person is the big kahuna at home, as researcher George Barna puts it. Now, I don't consider myself better or more important than anyone else. When our building crew installed a "Senior Pastor" parking spot close to our entrance, I refused to park in it. My parking spot is at the very edge of the parking lot—not up close to the front of the entrance. All leaders park a distance away and walk in. It is our way of messing with the notion that privilege comes with spiritual position. But, in fact, something powerful is communicated when the big kahuna of the church personally communicates with people visiting the church for the first time.

Handwrite a Note on Sunday Night

After all the services are done for the weekend, I use a nice fountain pen or a roller-type ballpoint pen to handwrite a personalized welcome letter to each newcomer family. I know it sounds like a lot of work, but this step in the follow-up of newcomers pays huge dividends. And I disagree with those who think it's too much work. Once you get in the groove of writing notes each Sunday evening, you will find it's doable and energizing even. Just think of all those amazing opportunities that are being forged as you write the letters.

On any Sunday evening, I might write notes to as many as several dozen newcomers. Usually I watch a movie or two to unwind from the weekend while I write these letters. Keep in mind that the letter is not long or complicated. A typical note might say:

> Dear Bob and Sally,
>   Glad you were with us. Hope you felt at home. Hope Bobby felt loved. I'd love to meet you. Please come up and introduce yourselves to me after a service sometime soon.
>   Sincerely,
>   Steve Sjogren
>
> P.S. Have some ice cream on me!

Usually people's eyes go right to a letter's postscript. In my letter, I include a coupon good for a scoop of ice cream at a good ice-cream place in town. Why ice cream? People smile when they think about eating it.

I address each envelope by hand, as well. This step is vital. When newcomers go through their mail, the first piece they will open is the most unusual one—the hand-addressed envelope. When they read the letter and realize that the pastor took the time to handwrite a note and address the envelope, they will be impressed. I have been in the homes of people who've been in our church for more than two years and found my handwritten letter on their refrigerator. It is clear that newcomers are impressed with the effort that's involved in a handwritten note.

Send the Letters on Monday
Mailing the handwritten letters on Monday means that newcomers will receive their letters on Tuesday while their visit to the church is still fresh in their minds.

Call Newcomers on Thursday

This call is strategically important. It should be very short and sweet, because it will come at a time when people are not expecting it. Since the call will be intruding on their schedule, it needs to be very short—less than five minutes. The objective of the call is simply to take the process to the next level. When I call, I say who I am and invite the newcomers out for pie. Pie is a happy food (kind of like ice cream). Everybody likes pie. It's nature's best food, as someone has famously said.

Take Them Out for Pie

When I invite the newcomers out for pie (or ice cream in a pinch), I promise that we will only be about 30 minutes. During the "pie time," I give a brief history of the church and a micro-perspective on where we are theologically ("Billy Graham wearing blue jeans and believing in the power of the Spirit"). Then I ask if they have any questions. I don't eat much pie, as you might guess! I have found that about 80 percent to 90 percent of those who have pie with me end up "sticking" with the church for two years or more. Most people are willing to connect with you for a long-term journey on the basis of being taken out for dessert. They will think long about leaving after having been shown that much consideration.

Ask Where They Fit In

It is only natural that you either do a simple spiritual gifts test or you simply ask the person where their passions lie. Until you have a group that is over 1,000 in size on weekends, it is not that difficult to understand how newcomers can fit into the system of needs. Make recommendations as to where people can fit into the system of needs in the church at large.

It is important that you explain to those who are working with newcomers in ministry how they will need to relate to volunteer helpers. Give them training initially and in an ongoing way to help them practice how to get along with volunteer help. Most volunteer workers have been dealt with in both positive and negative ways, so they know intuitively when things are being done well.

The *Process* of Inclusion

I have always been uncomfortable with models for including newcomers that are structured with stages for the newcomer to go through. You've likely seen those models. I find them unrealistic and limiting. They reflect a modern mindset rather than a postmodern approach that is more in touch with the sorts of people who are coming into my church.

It's a good thing to have an educational track in church, perhaps a class called Church 101 to be followed by a more advanced class called Church 201, which, in turn, would be followed by Church 301 and, finally, Church 401. Our goal should be fully devoted followers of Christ. But we mustn't confuse training with true spiritual maturity. One is information-based while the other is spiritual formation-based.

Newcomers' Pizza Class

We call our introductory class Newcomers' Pizza because we serve pizza to people who attend. The pizza is just an excuse to invite people. The real point of the time together is to get to know these new folks a bit and allow them to get to know the church a bit. Specifically, we want them to hear about the history of the church and about our theological "distinctives." People want to know who we are and where we are going as a church. The distinctives that make VCC somewhat unique are our worship and evangelism. To illustrate both, we show a clip from the movie *Sister Act.* We show the scene that starts with the choir singing in Latin then shifting to a more upbeat version in English. In the movie, Sister Mary Clarence (Whoopi Goldberg) gets into trouble for changing the choir's style. As Sister Mary Clarence is being reamed out for the unauthorized changes, the priest and the rest of the sisters barge in. Sister Mary Lazarus, who wears a hearing aid around her neck that looks like an older style portable transistor radio, perks up and says, "You know, sister, there's a lot more that we could do for the people than just pray for them." The video then shows the entire convent breaking out from behind the cloister walls, cutting down the chain-link fence and going into the community. The nuns begin to include the community in a dozen ways, and the church immediately begins to grow.

The moral behind this part of the film, and what we hope our newcomers walk away with, is that only as we break out of our cloistered lives can we begin to change the world. As we adjust our worship so that it's understandable for the average person, we will attract the attention of the watching world.

Invite people to the next step by offering other classes in addition to Newcomers' Pizza, such as "How to Get into a Small Group" and "How to Discover Your Gifts and Talents." Be sure to offer information on where people can serve in the church. In addition, I highly recommend the Alpha course: A 15-session, practical introduction to the Christian faith, it is designed to help seekers find relationship with Christ and to bring new believers into a solid relationship with Christ (see www.alpha course.org). After looking into this course you may end up adjusting it to your own style as we have. In any case, this is a brilliant combination of presenting spiritual truth with the sharing of food in the same experience week after week.

Joining VCC

Every church has a membership, whether that membership is spelled out and called such or not. It's just that some are formalized and some are not. We started out thinking we would not have a membership. Now that I've had adequate time to look back at the pros and cons of the issue, I wish we had gone for a formal membership from the get-go of our church's history. It would have clarified who was in and who wasn't. I'm not convinced that the decision to have a membership would have increased the overall commitment level, but it would have helped people qualify their relationship with the church—which would be helpful for both them and us.

In lieu of a formal membership, I developed an informal way of helping people know whether they were in or out of our ranks. If a person wants to be a part of VCC, he or she needs to connect at the following levels, and we help them do this:

1. *Find God* (Find salvation, then come faithfully on weekends and give to the cause financially so that we can go beyond what we are doing now around the city with other church start-ups that are happening with increasing frequency.)

2. *Find a friend* (Get committed to community/ group relationships.)

3. *Find a job* (Discover a ministry gift or talent and get involved by serving in one form or another as that becomes enjoyable to you through the process of discovery, trial and error.)

The Cycle of How We See People

Beyond an assimilation program, the way we see people guides everything. Acceptance allows people to be in process. Acceptance allows people to be in church even if they don't have it all together. In fact, it recognizes that no one has it all together—that we are all in process. One way to understand this constant state of process is to look at it as a cycle: from *hospital* to *family* to *school* to *army* then back to *hospital*. Let me explain.

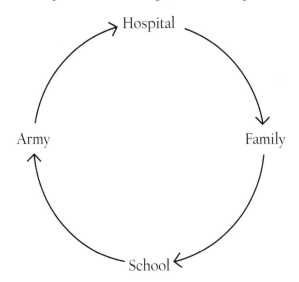

This model is different from the baseball-diamond model because it shows a person going through the cycle continuously. On the baseball diamond, a runner progresses to first base and then moves on to second base, never to return to first base. The runner moves from one base to the next to finally arrive at home plate. Theoretically, a runner stays at home plate indefinitely, fully equipped to do ministry. However, life doesn't work that way.

That view of humanity doesn't take into account the Jimmy Swaggart Syndrome. You're probably familiar with the sad story of his fall into immorality in the late 1980s. Though his life message had been, in part, one of holiness, he was caught twice in compromising situations with prostitutes. After the first situation, he apologized on television. During that much-replayed apology, he sobbed, "I have sinned!" His sorrow was obviously very sincere. Yet not long after the dust settled on that situation, he was found with another couple of prostitutes. Later, Swaggart admitted in interviews that he had quietly suffered through the shame of an addiction to pornography for decades, all the while conducting evangelistic crusades around the world.

Swaggart was stuck in a system that saw him as having arrived at maturity in Christ—at home plate in perpetuity. He had problems, even addictions, but his church system didn't encourage him to admit problems and ask for help.

The way that life and spirituality work is more like a cycle than a straight, linear path to perfection. In my analogy there is the Hospital, the Family, the School, and the Army.

Hospital

We are all born into the hospital. We all have hurts, needs, injuries and problems. The church needs to provide caring ministry and places where people can begin to heal, feel loved and work on their issues. These places might include classes to help people understand boundaries, dysfunctional families and addiction issues. Some people just need a place to rest and get reenergized after ministry burnout. When we are in the hospital, we are not yet ready to lead or serve. We shouldn't stay there forever, though; we need to cycle through the hospital.

Family

In the family, we find belonging and community, and we learn about Christ's unconditional love. As we immerse ourselves in small groups, we experience forgiveness and acceptance, and we learn to love without condition.

School

School trains us and equips us for life and ministry. This is where we develop our skills and become more effective for life overall. We are capable of doing all we had hoped for early on in life.

Army

The powers of darkness cringe at the awesome power of the light of the church as it is represented in fullness in the army of God. In the army, we do the work of the church: intercessory prayer, serving, leading and helping. But as we serve in the army, we can be wounded by the warfare.

Here's how the progression works. We move naturally from the hospital, or the caring ministries of the church, to where we become part of the family. The family embraces us in an atmosphere of acceptance and forgiveness, which prepares us for school. At school we learn about the unique ministries that God has given us. Once we are adequately equipped, we enter the army, where exciting ministry and warfare take place. But once we're in the army, it probably won't be long before we're wounded. Wounds wear us down until, eventually, we're unable to work effectively in the army of God, and we become dysfunctional. It is a mere matter of time until we are all periodically dysfunctional. In my opinion if we are not now and then dysfunctional, we are not availing ourselves to God hard enough.

That's when we have a need to return to the hospital for a visit to repair ourselves. Sometimes work in the army uncovers things from the past, and we need to work on those issues in particular. Whatever the problem, people should feel safe enough to admit they need the healing of the hospital from time to time. When the hospital has done its healing work, it's a good idea to delve more deeply into the family of small groups and then receive more training in school to avoid again making the ministry mistakes that put us in the hospital—if those were mistakes that put us in the hospital. Sometimes we end up in the hospital simply because we were taking risks that were necessary to take and we were the given person(s) to take them.

How to Be More Inclusive

• Redefine *evangelism* to mean "bringing and including."

• Establish a process for bringing newcomers into the life of your church, and diligently follow up on those new people God brings your direction.

• Develop a winsome system for greeting and ushering (you can develop your own system given that you understand what you are trying to see newcomers experience when they arrive at your front door).

- Observe the spiritual progress of those God is bringing you.

- Talk about inclusion with your team again and again and again—until that's all they think and give away. The success or failure of what we do rides on our ability to include newcomers in what we are doing. Without an inclusion mentality, we are all sunk.

- Find an Inclusion Cheerleader other than the senior leader. (Think of this person as an assistant evangelist for gathering and including—the senior leader must be the primary gatherer and includer always if your approach is to work.) Typically, a good candidate for the Inclusion Cheerleader will be an older person who is financially stable so that he or she will have the time to do the job. This person hopefully won't have a theological axe to grind. In our church, his name is Ron. Perhaps you have a "Ron" at your church just waiting to be identified. Give this book to the Ron at your church who wants to make newcomers feel warm and included. Ron can make others successful and can coach people in the church about how to be inclusive. Ron has the patience and heart and time to do the job. In addition to the contents of this book, there are free PDF articles available for reading and downloading at my website, Kindness Resources.com. Check that site frequently because I add to that storehouse on a regular basis.

Chapter 8

TRUSTING

Oh the inexpressible comfort of feeling safe with a person;
having neither to weigh thoughts nor to measure words,
but to pour them all out, just as they are, chaff and grain
together, knowing that a faithful hand will take and sift
them, keep what is worth keeping, and then, with the
breath of kindness, blow the rest away.

George Eliot

When it snows in Cincinnati, people freak out. Just a little of the white stuff causes them to stay indoors for the day. I wondered if I should cancel our small-group meeting this snowy night, but I had decided early on in the history of our church that we'd be like the mail delivery: Neither rain, nor sleet, nor snow would keep us from meeting. We have a rule now—we always meet, no matter what.

Our group of about a dozen people was about half that size that evening. My first impression was that it was going to be a slow night. It's difficult enough to get people to open up and share in a small group, much more so when the group is only six people.

But that night the subset of the small group bonded in a peculiar way. We experienced some of the community the Scriptures promise will happen when we gather as believers. Maybe we felt bonded because we had all braved the storm to be together. Whatever the cause, we all shared deeply that night. People opened up and shared dreams about the future. Some shared their fears about what might kill those dreams.

As we finished up that night, one woman said, "You know, this is as close to 'family' as I've ever had in my life. Tonight seems like as good a time as any to say that to you all. I just want to say thanks for your consistent willingness to be there for me." With hearts full of encouragement, people ventured out to brush off cars that had several more inches of snow piled on them and slowly made their way home. They all checked in when they made it home. Amazingly, no one got stuck in the snow.

It's been a few years since that snowy night, but it remains as clear as ever in my mind's eye. I think I will forever keep that inclement weather night in my heart. What happened demonstrated part of the reason I became a Christian—the hope that I, a dysfunctional person struggling through life, could find other dysfunctional people and that somehow, by the power of God, we could learn to get along. It's the hope that God has placed in my heart to know and experience the kingdom of God here on earth. When it happens, it is evidence that God is at work, because none of us can create that experience on our own apart from God.

Sin is my nature, the only thing I know how to do.
Brother Lawrence

To know and experience God's kingdom here on earth, we need to trust one another. By *trust*, I mean the willingness to come into community—to trust others enough to open up our lives to one another. Small groups aren't the only way to develop that kind of community, but they are the easiest and most direct method I know of.

Churches will never grow past a weekend attendance of 200 people until they get small—until they get into community through small groups. There is no better way to develop leaders. There is no better way to develop disciples who will understand and embrace the values of the Perfectly Imperfect Church than through the development of small-group leaders and small groups.[1]

A person's a person, no matter how small!
The philosopher Horton the Elephant

Like a Big Small Group

If your church has a weekend attendance of fewer than 200 people, the first thing you need to do to get small and create community is to go to two services. That move will develop the need for small groups. Small groups won't work unless you have two services, because your weekend service will serve as your small group.

I suggest having two services your first week together as a church. I coach all of my church planters to provide two services the first week of offering Sunday services, no matter how small the church is. Two services will break up the "we four and no more" clique mentality that is so common in small churches.

Once a group grows to more than 30 people, it is impossible to know everyone at a level deeper than merely knowing names. But people won't feel the need to gather in smaller groups until the group has divided into at least two smaller subsets.

If a small group is to survive, it must have some sort of outreach component. The fastest way to kill a small group is to make it an inwardly focused entity. I have seen many groups die from infighting over miniscule issues that likely could have been taken care of if there had simply been an outward element to the group.

I recommend that each small group define what a normal outreach schedule in their calendar of meetings should be. For example, if the group meets every week, planning outreach for every sixth meeting might be reasonable. Plan outreach projects that are simple and close to where the group meets. (See my book *101 Ways to Reach Your Community* for outreach project ideas.) Begin the outreach meeting together to talk briefly about what the outreach will be. Then go out for an hour to do the project. After the outreach project, bring the group together again to discuss how things went, and have some refreshments.

> **Feeling Kind of Kind—Fake Community**
> MDMA's ("Ecstasy") effect on the brain is to hyperstimulate the manufacture of serotonin. The torrent of serotonin that is unleashed brings about a state of consciousness in which it is difficult to feel anxious or depressed, or anything other than love and warmth and good will toward oneself and one's fellow human beings.

It is imperative that the senior leadership be involved in authentic relationships if the people of the church are to get involved as well. As the leaders do, so do the people. Too often I have seen senior leaders aspire to get the people in their congregations involved in small groups without actually being heartily involved in small groups themselves. There's no credibility in that leadership, and the leader's encouragement to get involved falls on deaf ears. Let your enthusiasm flow out of your own involvement and experience.

Before we can be greatly used by God, we must see the monstrous evil in our souls.
David Roper

How to Have a Great Small-Group Meeting

Start on Time
Reward the people who are on time by starting on time. Don't punish them by waiting for latecomers to show. Waiting for latecomers rewards and reinforces tardy behavior.

Open with a Preview
Say, "I'm glad you're here!" and explain what will happen. For example, you might say, "We'll worship with two or three songs. Then we'll share the good things God has been doing in our lives. Then we'll look at the Bible for a bit. At the end, you'll have time to share your prayer requests."

Worship
Worship is optional. Sing if your group enjoys it. Worship is good when it is good and not too stressful to pull off. To not

have music worship is not necessarily a gigantic loss. As someone has said, "The only thing worse than no worship is bad worship." I can think of a few things worse than no worship, but you get the point.

Share Ground Rules

Keep what's shared confidential. As we change and grow together, private things come to the surface in one another's lives. These occurrences and stories are confidential. It is obvious these ought never to be shared with those who are outside of the group, but some people need to be reminded that this information is strictly on a need to know basis.

No counseling of other group members. This may seem self-evident, but some people need to have this clarified for them each week or they will fall into the trap of explaining how they think others ought to live their lives in order to come into proper alignment.

No complaining about other churches. If you allow people to share their frustrations with their past church, you start to go down a dark trail that will discolor your meetings immediately. It only takes an itsy-bitsy complaint to put a bad taste in the mouths of everyone present.

The meeting will be done within one-and-a-half to two hours. If you want to hang out for a little bit, you can. But you are free to leave at that point. One role of the group leader is to monitor the length of stay of people. If some are staying longer than the welcome mat is set out, that needs to be addressed on a one-on-one basis.

Do Some Get-to-Know-You Stuff

The leader should have a vision for the group that includes helping people get to know each other. The classic activity is to have people introduce themselves and tell a little about themselves. The *Serendipity Bible* offers hundreds of open, safe questions that can help people begin to share and get to know one another. Another twist is to have people pair up to talk and then have each person share with the group about the person they talked with.

God-Is-Good Talk

Invite people to express to the group something good that God has been doing in their lives. Remind people to save prayer requests and needs for later. If people begin to get negative with their comments, take charge by saying, "We'll share our prayer needs later in the meeting. This is the time we share the good things the Lord is doing in our lives."

Do Your Study

Keep the study part simple so that studies can be used again as the groups reproduce. Use good discussion questions, and don't preach. Don't let anyone dominate the response time with a too-long response. Keep the study time interesting by encouraging a lot of people to contribute. It's fine to call upon people who aren't contributing by name and ask what they think of the question at hand. Some people will not share unless they are called upon.

Pray

Vary how the prayer time is done, but make it a time to bring up needs. One option is to stay together and pray as a group as long as the prayers are kept short. One-sentence prayers are great. Another option is to break into groups of three so people can pray for one another in the groups. One person in each group should be appointed the leader. The second option takes a little longer, so more time needs to be allotted for it.

If people pray in groups of three, remind everyone that it is a *prayer* time, not a counseling time.

Have Refreshments

Refreshments aren't essential, but serving something simple will encourage people to gather at the end of the meeting to talk and get to know each other. To keep provision of refreshments from becoming a burden on the host, encourage the group members to take turns bringing the refreshments.

The Makeup of a Small Group

Group Leader

The group needs a leader to pull the group together and keep things going.

Apprentice Leader

The apprentice may be the most important member of the group, because he or she will take the next group when the original group multiplies—something that should happen sooner rather than later. When you do increase the group by making two from the one, use the activating word "multiply," and never say "divide." When a healthy, enjoyable group is going in two different directions, it is a natural defensive reaction for one or more people to think the worst and become a person who can move against what God is up to in this situation. God is always on the move to multiply His love and life. He doesn't ever divide His people. He generates life by multiplying things on the high side.

Host and Hostess

The host and hostess open their home to the group and create an environment that is warm and inviting for all. With good hosting, a group will thrive. Without it, it will not grow. The home you choose for your meeting should be easy to find. I've been in groups that met in homes that were great *once you got there*, but the homes were almost impossible to find and, therefore, not the best choice. Also consider parking, the noise level in the home and any other distractions. Where childcare is a concern, consider hiring a reliable neighbor to watch children in her home. Teenagers that you know and trust can also be good choices for childcare, but the children should not be in the home where the meeting is held.

Worship Leader

I see worship as an option, and by no means a necessity, but it is a great addition if you can do it well. Small-group worship almost has to be done with guitar accompaniment, considering the limitations of mobility and people's skills (it's difficult to sing and play the trombone at the same time!). Worship should be short and sweet—no more than 15 minutes if you are keeping to the hour-and-a-half to two-hour schedule.

Outreach Leader

The outreach leader is a cheerleader who keeps the group looking outward. Not all of your outreaches will go smoothly or seem successful, so the outreach leader should be someone with an indomitable spirit that keeps on keeping on in spite of the odds. This person also needs to be creative and able to work with little to make much, because there will be less-than-ideal situations as you prepare to go out to do outreach.

How to Reproduce Small Groups En Masse ("Turbo-Groups")

Thank about small-group expansion and reproduction as soon as you begin to form your small-group system. To prepare for expansion, I've developed turbo-groups to train several group leaders at once in a relatively short time. Over the years, I have had great success using turbo-groups to train lots of small-group leaders.

You can easily judge the character of others by how they treat those who can do nothing for them or to them.
Malcolm Forbes

I train leaders and then place their names in a "ready-to-go" pool. These potential leaders are told upfront that they will not necessarily be given a group to lead upon the completion of the training period. I allow practically anyone who has a desire to be trained to take the small-group training. I offer the training based on the let-the-cream-rise-to-the-top principle. Those who are the best budding small-group leaders will be apparent by the end of the training period.

The most profound movie I've viewed in the past few years is *Freaks,* a 1932 film starring circus sideshow folk. In today's politically correct vernacular, we would call them "special needs" people. The characters in this film have profound physical disabilities. Some are hard to believe even when you see them. (The film was banned in England for decades because the physical disabilities it shows are so disturbing. Some of the characters appear to be filmed with special effects, but then you remember it was shot in 1932, in black and white, long before that was a possibility.)

When you stand at the Pearly Gates,
would you rather be told that you were too
forgiving or you were too judgmental?
Leonard Sweet

The movie has had such an impact on me that I'm a bit of a *Freaks* salesman; I'll show it to anyone who expresses the least bit of interest in its message. Though the self-named freaks face incredible difficulties on a daily basis, none of them chooses to sink into self-pity for even a minute. (Without ruining the story for you, it's the "normal" people who are the real "freaks," as it turns out.) These sideshow folks find great joy and satisfaction in simple lives lived in authentic community. Their basic needs are met as they do what they love, which is working together in the circus. They get through life and are fulfilled because, more than anything else, they have one another. The film presents a compelling picture of a trusting community—a picture that I think is close to the imprint for belonging that God has placed in all of our hearts.

Note

1. When I use the term "small group," I'm talking about the entire range of community-building mechanisms. I believe that traditional small groups, as they are typically understood, do not work well with certain age groups—Generation X people, for example, who seem to typically prefer to not meet in homes in small numbers. In some ways, the way we think of small groups is more of a Baby Boomer idea. It is the best mechanism we have at hand now, but the bottom line is that we need to learn new ways of developing authentic community, in whatever form it takes.

Chapter 9

ATMOSPHERIC

I recently visited two cathedrals. They represented vastly different theological perspectives. One was the historic national cathedral on Mexico City's city square. The building is so old that it's beginning to sink into the lakebed it was built on hundreds of years ago.

I walked in during a Saturday night mass and saw a sanctuary filled with the soft light from hundreds of votive candles lit by the worshipers. With my limited Spanish, I understood about every tenth word, and I heard frequent references to "Maria." During my 30-minute stay, I observed how people sang their way through the Roman Catholic mass with great gusto. It was clear that these people loved God the Father and His Son, Jesus. While I disagree with much of the theological content of the Roman Catholic message, I believe that Catholics are brothers and sisters in Christ (they believe more than I do, not less). I sensed the presence of the Holy Spirit at that service.

Contrast that scene with another cathedral I visited in Bern, Switzerland. This historic site was at the center of several Reformation events. The Word of God has been faithfully proclaimed there and continues to be to this day. While these Reformed people may be technicians of God's Word, I'm sure they don't realize the vibes they give off. My experience there was absolutely antithetical to the love and warmth I find in the grace of Christ. From the brusque tour guides who unemotionally explained the history of the building in hushed tones, to the chilly room temperature, the entire experience would have been a turnoff to any not-yet-Christian contemplating the possibility of following Christ. I dare say the people at that cathedral may possibly be doing more damage than good to the cause of Christ.

No doubt, as some of you are reading these sentences, a verse from Isaiah is flashing through your minds: "My word . . . will not return to me empty, but will accomplish what I desire" (Isa. 55:11). Yes, that's true. Praise God that's true; because, in light of the often pathetic job the church has done in creating an atmosphere that is conducive to attracting outsiders, we might otherwise have no fruit whatsoever. But we can do much better!

Those two places of worship—the cathedrals in Mexico City and in Bern—are studies in atmospheric contrasts: One had a not-so-biblical belief system but a great atmosphere; the other had a very precise and unquestionably biblical belief but a deadly atmosphere. We don't have to choose between those two extremes; we can have right beliefs and a fantastic atmosphere that is conducive to embracing those beliefs.

One of our servant evangelism projects is to give away popsicles. Our church has its own popsicle truck, complete with children's music. It's just like the ice-cream trucks you grew up with—equipped with special hydraulics that allow it to bounce when it's driven, our truck draws a crowd wherever it is parked. We create an atmosphere that's larger than the mere elements of the truck and the treats it contains. The ice-cream truck builds a presence. Its atmosphere is complete with sights, sounds and tastes.

We stole the show at a local parade by driving the truck at the end of the parade, just after a battalion of motorcyclists in full regalia. The truck bounced along, playing its music and distributing thousands of popsicles to hot parade watchers.

Atmosphere Architects

We are all called to be atmosphere architects in God's kingdom. The senior leader is to be the prime architect of your church. His or her job includes oversight of the weekend celebration experience, as well as leading people to experiences in generosity, outreach and community. With a watchful eye, the architect applies the glue that holds the atmosphere together.

We were sponsoring a "Free, No Kidding, Car Wash" one Saturday. I was serving as the atmosphere architect that morning, tending to all the details that go into making a car wash a party and not a funeral. I've learned that the best cars are the last cars of the day. Today was no exception. A woman pulled in near the end of the day, and as she got out of her car, I had a sense that she was burdened emotionally. As her car was being tended to, I asked if she had any prayer needs. As is typical when I ask that question, she said she was doing just fine. So I rephrased my question. I asked, "If Jesus were standing here right now, what would you ask Him to do for you?"

She said, "Oh, that's different. I'd ask Him to free me from my grief. You see, my grandma, whom I was very close to, died a week ago today. In fact, I've been thinking about her all day today. I miss her terribly." I asked if she would mind if I prayed for her, and she said she would appreciate it. Judging by her response, I suspect she pictured me praying at the end of the day, with a prayer something like, "Now I lay me down to sleep . . . and God bless that lady at the car wash." But I meant I would pray for her right on the spot. So I did.

Often, when people are served, they respond to things in an emotional way; so over the years, I've come up with a *tear meter,* an emotional response rating system. It runs from 1 to 10.

A level 1 on the scale is the manly tear that brims in the eye but doesn't quite trickle down the cheek. I have found that only men are capable of such tears. Generally, when women cry, they jump right into a higher level on the scale. This seems like a good thing. (Again, in general, women seem to be more in touch with their emotions in a positive way than most men. Most men work on not showing their emotions even though they deeply feel their emotions in a big way.)

A level 3 tear trickles partway down the cheek but evaporates before it hits the chin. Level 5 tears actually drip off the chin on both sides of the face. At level 7, both the tears and the nose are engaged at the same time. You might wonder if there is actually a level 10 on this scale. There is, though I've only seen it a couple of times. At level 10, a person is so emotionally engaged that the tears actually jump off his or her face horizontally instead of dropping vertically. It's quite a sight.

As I began to pray for the woman at the car wash and ask the Holy Spirit to relieve some of her pain, she began to cry profusely. She went right into level 7 tears. It was beautiful. The Lord touched her when she was least expecting it. The best part was that it happened outdoors at a busy gas station. Though the external atmosphere was far from ideal, God created a just-right spiritual environment that worked fine.

All churches create an atmosphere. "Atmosphere," as used here, is what people feel in a church. It's not the left-brain, linear programs. It's not the things that are seen, but the unseen. Those unseen intangibles are speaking volumes to your attendees and are especially noticeable to newcomers.

Tuning your attention to the atmosphere means learning to notice things you wouldn't normally notice. Many elements make up the atmosphere at the mall. However, because you have been to the mall many times, you take that environment for granted. If those elements—as subtle as they are—were missing, you would notice that the mall just wasn't the same.

In the same way, we need to attune ourselves to building and maintaining a warm and inviting atmosphere that works with our vision for what church should be.

> **God's Kingdom Is an Atmosphere**
> Craig Van Gelder wrote that the kingdom of God isn't a place as much as it is what I call an atmosphere. According to Van Gelder, "The basic idea of the kingdom is that God in Jesus powerfully entered human history with a reign that reestablished life on the basis of redemptive power." The kingdom of God, he said, is about the "dynamic presence of God's redemptive power confronting the forces of evil and restoring life to its fullness."[1]

Fine-tuning the Atmosphere

Consider some of these adjustments to the atmosphere you are creating in your church.

Atmosphere Adjustment: Coffee in the Sanctuary

I know, some of you are gasping for breath right now. "Coffee in the sanctuary?! That would never fly at our church." I had that same reaction when this idea first surfaced, but there is nothing more powerful in changing the atmosphere of your church than to allow coffee (with lids!) into your sanctuary. Some would say, "But what about the carpet? We'll soil it!" Coffee is a community-building drink. No matter what possible mess is created (we've allowed coffee for years and have had relatively few accidents), it's well worth the trouble for the atmosphere that it creates.

Atmospheric Adjustment: Lighting

Stage lighting is vital for the creation of a great atmosphere. Lights are an investment up front, but they are well worth it when installed and controlled properly with gel filters. There are only a few things that can be totally controlled in the auditorium environment. The lights are one of them.

For the congregation, we have found that softer lighting during worship works well. We increase the lighting as needed for people to take notes or read from their programs. In my travels throughout the Church in the West, I have found that nearly all churches could double their current lighting situation and do well for it.

Atmosphere Adjustment: Color

If you have inherited a vintage building, you probably have some interesting color schemes to work with. No matter what your building inheritance situation (the facility you have to work with—whether you have received it or you have discovered it along the way), there is a need for upgrading your facility's color schemes on a fairly regular basis simply to keep up with the times. For the most part, even a horrendous color problem can be solved with new carpeting and a coat of paint. Empower your "design team" to submit a few color schemes to keep your environment fresh and inviting. Think of the paradigm "inviting family room" versus "formal living room." For ideas, look at a few newer hotel lobbies that use designers to create an atmosphere where people want to come and stay. It is not necessarily essential that you go to the expense of hiring a decorator. The key point is to keep your renovations in sync with your long-term plans.

Keep in mind that you communicate value to the people coming as you take the time and energy to create a truly welcoming space for them.

Atmosphere Adjustment: Pace and Flow
Is there a sense of nervousness to your services or a relaxed flow? Adjust your transitions and make your service flow comfortably. The way you come across has everything to do with how you communicate internally with your team.

Atmosphere Adjustment: Before and After
Just as Muzak is played at the mall to create an atmosphere, we play decent worship music as people are entering and leaving our facility. It puts people who are arriving into a mode of worship. Many who are walking into the facility are not doing well emotionally; they need all the encouragement they can get.

Atmosphere Adjustment: Stage Appearance
Your people have to look at the front of your stage for at least an hour each weekend. They will notice little things, daydream and count the bricks, but hopefully pay attention to the excellent teaching. What does your stage say?

Is your stage cluttered? Are cords strewn all over? Is the overall look inviting or chaotic? Is the appearance of your people on stage like the rest of the people who attend the church or do they wear special clothing that sets them apart (a negative in my mind). Women should be conscious of their clothing, that is, not too tight and not too short, as a stage is usually set higher than the congregation. Provide a full-length mirror backstage so musicians, singers and speakers can make sure everything is in order.

Atmosphere Adjustment: Minimize Distractions

Empower your ushers (hosts, greeters, elders, helpers—whatever you call them) to help minimize distractions from any source. For example, sometimes a mother sitting in a service is oblivious to the sounds her fussy baby or bored preschooler is constantly making. She has grown accustomed to a certain noise level and is thrilled to be out of the house. Another mom may be mortified that her child is noisy, but stays frozen in her seat to avoid creating a further scene by leaving.

In either case, the usher can politely ask, "Would you mind standing in the back? The baby's/child's noises are distracting to others." If you have a cry room, you could say, "We have a room with a TV monitor just for mothers in this situation so they can remove distraction but not miss any of the service. May I show you where that room is?" (I have found that a female usher making that request is far better received than a male.) A cry room, TV monitors in the hallways, sugarless suckers, crayons and coloring sheets are all possible helps to the situation. Although you risk offending a mother and her "perfect" child, you are sure to offend many by doing nothing.

Atmosphere Adjustment: Temperature

Is it too warm or too cold? Usually the problem is that it's too warm. It's difficult to pay attention to the message when it's difficult to stay awake. Airflow follows along with a comfortable air temperature. As long as somewhat fresh air is flowing, it is possible to stay alert in a closed room. But it is challenging to stay alert in a room that is on the warm side.

If you have a smallish environment, stay away from any openness that indicates you are willing to take orders to adjust the room temperature. Find a middle-aged man of medium build to be in charge of the temperature. Such a person is not going to go through hot flashes. He is not going to be manipulated by the crowd, half of which want to be warmer, half of which want to be cooler. Trust in his capacity to keep the room on the cool side.

Atmosphere Adjustment: Seating

This is the third element that can be controlled, in addition to lighting and temperature. Is your seating comfortable? Is it easy to get to? Do you have flexible seating? Is the spacing adequate so that you aren't frustrating people?

How to Build Atmosphere

- *Good atmosphere means saying no to certain things.* Say yes to the things that will allow the atmosphere to flourish. Say no to what will impede that vision from being realized. It is only natural that you will say no to far more things than you will say yes to as you realistically look at the schedule. It is impossible to move forward and say yes to an unending list of seemingly good ideas. As you look at a possible idea, the church leadership must discern what it is that you will involve yourselves with in the coming days and months. You cannot do all things. But you can do a number of things that are exciting and worthwhile. Those are the things that God has put on your plate to experience and focus upon.

• *Analyze your services.* Consider hiring "secret shoppers": pay $30 to someone to come and give their honest opinion about what they experience. You need the details about the atmosphere that they can offer you.

• *Surround yourself with the right people.* The right people can greatly affect atmosphere; the contrary is accurate as well. Make sure that you are not surrounded by the wrong people who can negatively affect your atmosphere. Spending lots of time with downer people makes things very difficult if not impossible to pull off. Sometimes it is difficult to get rid of the wrong people. The easier task is to add positive people to your team.

• *Pay attention to who's answering the phone at your church.* This may seem like a small thing, but you would be surprised at how big a difference this will make when it is finally taken care of after an extended time of the wrong person answering the phone. The person who answers the phone is your first connection to the watching world. You are projecting your image to countless people on a daily basis through the voice and mannerisms of someone who may not even enjoy the job he or she has—that of connecting with the public at large and representing your organization. Are they conveying the atmosphere you want them to? Are they part of the solution, or are they furthering the problem? By the way, did you know that people can hear a smile over the phone? Try it yourself by calling a friend or your spouse and ask if they can hear the difference. Guaranteed, they will be able to hear the difference a smile makes when you project yourself properly on the phone.

- *Allow room for mistakes.* Don't demand that people be perfect up front. On the other hand, when someone has been in a position for an extended time and they continue to project a negative image, you may be doing them a favor by simply asking if they are in the right place in the organization. They might become overjoyed at the opportunity to move from Point A on to a better fit with things under the same roof. Or perhaps they no longer notice the negative image they have been projecting for so long.

- *Be bold!* Remember, you're leading a movement of change that is underway. Expect change and help your people to expect it.

- *Atmosphere is greater than the sum of its parts.* Atmosphere is worth guarding. It's holy. It's what makes this thing go forward. It's the nuclear-powered engine of all that you are doing.

- *Conduct weekly staff meetings as though you were already a great church in size and focus.* Reiterate the dream and vision continually. Be patient in restating the notion of where you are headed as a staff and leadership. The majority of people you are explaining this to have a lot of unlearning to do. Working with people in this setting is much like working with children who are open to learning but need a lot of nurturing of the basic idea of where you are headed. Smile as you do your restating of things. There is no point in getting mad at the sheep.

- *Build expectation.* Anticipate that when you get together something great is going to happen. Anything is possible when God shows up. God is present among His people and there's no telling what will happen as His power and presence are manifest. It is a role of leadership to increase the anticipation level among the people as they gather together. One aspect of faith is the anticipation of something great happening as the people of God gather together. If that's not happening sufficiently right now, perhaps it is time for leadership to pull aside and prayerfully listen to God's Spirit as He whispers what it is that He is about to do in your midst—or what it is that He desires to do in your midst in a big way.

- *Begin now to create the atmosphere you want to see in the future, then work backwards to make it happen.* The more writing you can do to clarify the great church you are erecting, the better. It will be necessary to write as much as you can about this amazing thing God and you are seeing come together.

• *Don't become overstressed about details and miss the big picture of what God is doing in your midst.* It's possible to go overboard to make every single aspect of your services neatly fit into your airtight view of how a celebration ought to go. While you pay attention to details, always keep the big picture in view.

Take Advantage of the Atmosphere God Has Created

We do all we can in terms of atmosphere building and negotiation. But when all is said and done, it is God and God alone who is the atmosphere architect. He alone can do something in an atmosphere that can cause something to happen in people's hearts. It is an enormous mistake to begin to think that we as leaders are the ones who are pulling the strings on people to cause them to do something or react in a certain way. Only God can change a heart. He can cause people to pick up on the differences that make a change. There is a subtle difference between preparation that is thorough and people who are taking credit for what God alone can do. Yes, let's thoroughly prepare, but let us be amazingly open to giving the credit to God for what is going on at all times.

Note

1. Craig Van Gelder, *The Essence of the Church* (Grand Rapids, MI: Baker Books, 2000), p. 75.

Chapter 10

GENEROUS

The night of the event, the place was buzzing. The room was jam-packed, with standing room only. There were so many people that I felt a little claustrophobic.

Let me backtrack a little. VCC was about to move into a new, multimillion-dollar facility, but we still needed several hundred thousand dollars for our real estate deal to go through. We had planned on using the money from the sale of our old facility to help finance the new one—until we felt that the Lord was showing us to do something completely counter to logic.

We had tried to sell the building for several months but had found no serious interest. As we prayed about the situation, we began to feel that the reason the building wasn't selling was that we were not to sell the building. We came to believe that we were to give the building away. God confirmed to me and to others that we were to give the church to a growing African-American church that was very interested but couldn't afford it. It didn't make sense logically speaking. We were struggling ourselves to come up with enough money to get into our new facility. What were we thinking with this crazy idea of giving away a building that was worth a million dollars? To top it off, we didn't fully own the building we wanted to give away. Though we had been in that facility for a number of years, we had never made it a priority to pay it off. We owed about $850,000.

I shared with our congregation the idea of giving away the building, and people went wild with excitement! We all agreed to keep it a secret from the other church while we all gave sacrificially for the next six weeks. We agreed to have a joint baptism service with the other church at the end of six weeks, on Good Friday, to spring the surprise on them.

The money came in spurts, and it came in amazing forms. People sold things that were meaningful to them to raise the cash we needed. Children made art and sold it. People sold their vacation homes. One woman sold the Barbie doll collection she'd built up since childhood. We received motorcycles, cars, boats, RVs, guns and a nighttime spying device (we didn't ask too many questions about where our donations came from).

A few days before the big night, we were still more than $100,000 short of our goal of the nearly $1 million needed. It seemed that people had given all they could give. So a few days before the due date, several of the pastors and I decided to hold a vigil. We announced that we would be at the church for 24 hours straight and that if people wanted to stop by and either pray or give money, they were welcome. What happened was amazing. There was a steady flow of people throughout that 24 hours. Some people dropped off more materials they wanted to donate. People dropped off lots of checks. Some stopped by to sit in the auditorium in stillness in the middle of the night.

One of the last to stop by was a little boy on his way to school. His mother dropped him off, and in he walked with a piggy bank full of change. He said he had been saving it to give to Jesus. When we tallied it all up—including what the little boy gave at the last minute—the total was right around $850,000—just what we needed to pay off the building debt.

When the big night arrived, we printed up a 2-foot-by-4-foot check for the gift amount. The church receiving the building was completely surprised. Some of the choir people actually fainted when the announcement was made! People in our church felt such an adrenaline rush that later many told me they couldn't sleep that night. When everything was said and done, when the lights were turned off and the last cars drove out of the parking lot, I was the last to leave. The building was no longer ours—and it felt great.

Generosity Is...

After experimenting with the power of generosity for the past few years, I have come up with a theology of generosity. I don't recall ever seeing such a theology in print before. It's not complicated, but it is biblical, and it works. Here are the components of my theology of generosity.

Generosity Is Uncanny

As a friend puts it, "Our commitment to generosity has to be freaky!" Generosity isn't something you can dabble in; it's a lifestyle to be embraced. There's no middle of the road. You're a person who embraces generosity or you're a person who doesn't. Generosity comes from the work of the Holy Spirit in our lives. It's better caught than taught.

Generosity Is Larger than Life

Generosity is larger than the key concept of outreach, and it is bigger than the matter of fun. It's the most important of all the concepts of the church that is great. It's the fountainhead of it all when it comes to having a heart for God's kingdom.

Generosity Is Contagious

When one or two people hop on board with the practice of generosity, more are sure to catch the raw excitement. When we gave our building away, not everyone was thrilled with the idea at first. After a few weeks, though, it was impossible to not be stoked about the project. People later told me they became impulse givers (similar to impulse shoppers, but in a positive sense) because they were swept up in the excitement of it all.

Generosity Compels Us to Give to Those Different from Us

The natural inclination is to give to people who are like us. We want to give only to those who are "worthy" or who "think right." But the power of generosity compels us to reach out beyond the comfort of our own lives and into the lives of those who are different from us. The church we gave our facility to was a black congregation. Cincinnati is a fairly segregated city, so the idea of giving to this group was no doubt a stretch for some people. But by the end, giving to that congregation was an overwhelming joy. We remain closely affiliated with that congregation today.

Generosity Is an Adventure

Generosity is an adventure like no other. We sow seeds and we wait to see what will grow. We do our part, and we trust God to bring fruit in His timing. It's energizing to see what God will do!

Adventures tend to write themselves as the stories continue forward. We can live the adventures and then write about them as things take place. We plant seeds, and then we watch to see what God does with the seeds we have seen spring up as they go their way.

Generosity that Seems to be Upside-Down Is the Norm

Giving away freely seems ludicrous to those who are not in the kingdom of God; but we are really right-side-up.

What Can You Do Today?

In an editorial piece written for *Newsweek* magazine, Jack McConnell described gathering around the dining-room table with his brothers and sisters. At every meal, his father, a Methodist minister, would ask each of the seven children, "And what did you do for someone today?"

Many years later, McConnell remembered his father's question. After a successful career in medical research, he and his wife retired to a home on Hilton Head Island, South Carolina. The home was in a gated community amid yacht clubs and golf courses. Beyond the gated community, though, native islanders lived a very different existence. Among the necessities of life these gardeners, maids and construction workers did without was medical care.

McConnell decided to do something for someone. With the help of other retired doctors on the island, he started a clinic to provide free primary health care to people in need of it. He convinced the state legislature to come up with a special license for volunteer doctors in not-for-profit clinics and found reasonable malpractice insurance. The town donated the land, and residents donated supplies. In 1994, the clinic opened. It logged 5,000 patient visits that year. In 2008, it logged 12,000 active patients, which equates to 30,000 patient visits annually. Other Volunteers in Medicine (VIM) clinics have opened around the country, all staffed by those who understand that it is better to give than to receive.[1]

Generating Generosity

Our churches need to be known for generosity outside the church walls, as well as inside them. Christian generosity has typically been aimed at others within the church walls. We must export our generosity in big, audacious ways that will grab the imaginations of the people around us. When outsiders think of us, what should automatically come to mind are people freely giving of their money, energy and gifts to make our cities and towns better places. Our goal is to cause people to smile when they hear about the latest venture, our most recent sacrificial hit of generosity. We need to have people think, *These guys really go the extra mile, don't they?*

All you need to get started are some good ideas. The following are some "Generosity Generators" to get you going. I recommend that, as you read these, you write your own ideas in the margin as they come to you.

Generosity Generator:
As a Church Body, Start with Percentage Giving

Begin to grow in generosity by disciplining yourself to designate a certain percentage of your church's budget to be given to others. I recommend starting by dedicating 3 to 5 percent of your budget to local outreach. However, the main thing is to *start with something* set aside for generous outreach efforts.

You've probably heard the term "tithes and offerings" as in, "Let's take up our tithes and offerings" during a weekend service. The "offerings" part of that phrase refers to giving beyond what a person normally gives to the local church. I recommend that you start a special offering fund and use it only for special financial needs in your community.

Generosity Generator:
Every So Often, Be Outlandishly Generous

VCC has been sending teams to Mexico City's dumps to minister to the people who make their living recycling what they find there. These people have many medical needs. Our teams spend about 10 days at a time ministering to these folks. The trips cost about $1,000 per person.

One weekend, as I encouraged people to give this mission a try, I offered to personally pay the first $100 if anyone needed help with raising the money for the trip. It was a spontaneous idea; I probably should have asked my wife before I made the offer! But then, I didn't expect 32 people to take me up on it! Janie understands about my spontaneous ideas and took the event in stride. At the same time, some 35 people came forward during the following week, without any prompting, and gave $100 each toward the project!

Generosity Generator:
Start a $20 Giveaway Challenge

Challenge the people in your church to see what they can do with $20 in one week. Whether the church provides the money or people provide their own start-up money, the idea is to challenge people in the church to use that money in a generous outreach idea that will touch as many people as possible. Give general instructions, including "be wise, be legal and be a servant in whatever you do." At the end of the week, gather the stories from the participants and share them the following weekend to encourage your church and spread the excitement about generosity.

Generosity Generator:
Practice Generosity by Tipping Well

As I mentioned earlier, we need to change the perception that restaurant workers have of Christians. Each time we eat out, we participate in a lab experiment—a chance to grow in generosity.

Typically, customers who don't drink alcohol don't tip as well as customers who do drink alcohol. When I don't order an alcoholic drink, the servers look a little downcast. I often ask, "So, what's your best tip of the day?" I tell them, "I may drink iced tea, but I tip like Jimmy Buffet."

> **Generosity in Tipping**
>
> Debra Ginsberg, author of *Waiting: The True Confessions of a Waitress*, wrote, "Every waiter and waitress I've worked beside agrees that almost everyone from the East Coast can be counted on for a good tip. They also agree that Europeans are the very worst tippers. I've actually seen fights break out over which country, France or Germany, has the cheapest diners."[2]
>
> French women with a bunch of kids in tow are the worst tippers imaginable. Why? They never learned to tip. They have never had a model. From my extensive experience of living and traveling in Europe, I know that tipping is rare (I've been told more than once, "In our country, tipping is illegal." I suspect they hadn't spoken with the waitresses on that issue!). The lesson in all of this? We all need a model for generosity. Someone has to show us the way first. We learn from those who model the way for us.

Tipping the Scales

A church in Charleston, South Carolina, conducted an experiment in generosity toward restaurant servers in the area. They tipped generously in restaurants around the city, and when they tipped, they left a card that read, "It's time for some change!" They filled the city with these cards, reshaping the way Charlestonians saw tipping and generosity.

Triple Tipping

I have discovered that across the board it has become increasingly common to tip just 10 percent, even for good service. No matter what happens during the exchange at a meal, it seems predictable that the tip will remain the same—a mere one-tenth of what the bill turns out to be. I have been working on stirring up a new definition of normal when it comes to tipping. I call it "Triple Tipping." That is, we give 30 percent of the bill back in the form of a tip. The normal response to normal service must be redefined by those of us who are up for a bit of a challenge. We must be the people who take responsibility to live out lives of generosity at the head of the people pack. Our part is to show the love of God in practical ways. We are the ones who must show the way. We are the "Talking-Doing" people. We don't just talk about what is the right thing to do, but we also do it and then talk about what we have done in retrospect as we enjoy the moment in reflection. We have a great time knowing that we are leading the way forward for others as they do what is right.

Few of us are strong enough that we can do something in a corner of humanity all by ourselves. We need the strength of others who are followers of the way of generosity as well. Thus is the power of connectivity and modeling the way onward.

Generosity Generator:
Build an Abundance Mentality

If you have a deprivation mentality, you can't give. When you have a conviction that to give is beyond your means, you can't afford to give because you won't have enough left over for yourself, or so you think. It may be that you just need to redefine what you can afford. A rich person isn't one who has the most stuff; a rich person is one who can give the most and thus live with the least to be fulfilled.

If you are lonely, I will call
I love you
I am the milkman of human kindness.
I'll leave an extra pint.

Billy Bragg
British punk rock pioneer[3]

Generosity Generator:
Give What You Need

We needed money to buy a piece of land. We had some of the money, but not nearly enough to make the down payment. The Christmas season was approaching, so we also needed a significant amount of cash for a huge free gift-wrapping project we had planned for the days before Christmas at a local mall.

However, we learned of another church that was also building a facility. We challenged people in our church to give to that church *before* they began to give to our church's property fund. With just a few days' notice, our church gave a surprise check for about $35,000 to the other church. By the following summer, we not only paid our down payment, but we were also able to burn the mortgage at our annual church picnic.

Generosity Generator:
Give What You Don't Have, and God Will Give
What You Could Never Produce for Yourself

God is in the business of multiplying back to us what we offer to Him. Make your resources available and God will repay you in ways that you can't imagine.

Generosity Generator:
Experiment with Giving in Outlandish
Ways Beyond Yourself

Remember that in the theology of generosity, generosity is a sport. Every once in a while we need to do something outlandish.

My friend Pastor Denny Bellesi at Coast Hills Community Church in Orange County, California, came up with an amazing idea. He called 100 random people in the congregation to come forward and gave each of them a $100 bill to invest in the community during a 90-day period. His idea was to encourage them to find creative ways to live out the parable of the talents. Once the church's money was handed out, the creativity started to flow. One of the $100-bill recipients told his men's group about the project, and by the end of the meeting, that single bill had turned into $2,300 for outreach funds. Another man invited four friends to dinner: a Christian, a Jew, a Buddhist and an agnostic. He divided the $100 among them. The Christian and the agnostic teamed up and raised $1,500 to send children with cancer to camp. The Buddhist bought coats, gloves and hats for homeless people. The Jewish woman raised another $50 and bought $75 worth of McDonald's hamburgers for a homeless shelter. When the manager heard about the project, she threw in hot apple pies.

At last count the original $10,000 has turned into $150,000—a small investment with a fabulous return. That's the business we're in!

Generosity Generator:
Take a Risk When You Can't See
the Way Forward

Even when you can't see the specific outcome, pray for courage, perseverance and a risk-taking attitude. The rewards for those who risk are great and far more worth stepping out for.

Give It Away!
A big money gift is weighing heavily on members of a small church. St. Mary's United Methodist Church in St. Mary's, Washington, received a gift of $60 million last month, enough to pay its annual budget for the next 210 years, according to news reports. Warren Bailey, who

attended the church as a child, left the money when he died at age 88. Parishioners and church leaders are at a loss for what to do with it. "Having that much money can have a negative impact on any church," Thomas Turner, a Baptist minister said. "I'm glad I don't have to deal with it."

How to Increase the Level of Generosity at Your Church

- Every once in a while—maybe on Mother's Day—take up an offering and give it away to another church or ministry that is in need. Great plans are carried out by great churches.

- Tap into people's unique desires to give. If you only have one way for people to give, you are limiting people's giving opportunities. Have different projects people can give to, ways you can pull on their heartstrings. For example, requested year-end giving probably ought not to be for the facility fund, but for something to the poor that will have a natural appeal.

Generous

For once in your life turn to your neighbor, pull out their wallet or purse, reach into the section where the money, credit cards and checks are located. Now give like you've always wanted to!
Line used in a giving campaign

We tend to learn to give from those around us.

Generosity of life is a learned behavior.

There is a spiritual gift of giving.

There is a spiritual discipline of generosity.

Sometimes generosity is confused with exploits of silliness that take place in spiritual institutions.

Notes

1. Jack McConnell, MD, "And What Did You Do for Someone Today?" *Newsweek* (June 18, 2001), p. 12; see also www.volunteersinmedicine.org/.

2. Debra Ginsberg, *Waiting: The True Confessions of a Waitress* (New York: HarperCollins, 2000), p. 40.

3. Billy Bragg, *The Milkman of Human Kindness* (London: Chappell Music Ltd., 1983).

Chapter II

TRUE

The two of us were having dinner at a Southern California restaurant and were kidding around. At least, I thought this pastor of a prominent church was kidding. In fact, I had just taken a sip of tea and I nearly spit it out I was laughing so hard. But he wasn't laughing.

The words hung in the air: "I could never have fellowship with you because you don't hold to the same view of the end times as me. That's too bad, because I like you as a friend."

He didn't know it, but at that point, I actually did hold to the same viewpoint as he did. But I was so grieved by his attitude of hairsplitting what I saw as miniscule issues that I didn't have the heart to tell him that we actually agreed.

Even though he was my friend, I felt as if I were talking to a church lawyer. I agreed with this pastor's theological perspective, but he was willing to write me off because I violated his religious tradition.

True: Essentials, Traditions, Opinions

I've been doing some thinking since that time. I've been thinking about what's important and what's not so important. As I see it, there are levels of issues. The first layer is absolutely vital. I call this the *Essentials*. Without agreement on these matters, we actually aren't even believers aligned with the Church and its past 2,000 years of history.

Beyond the essentials are *Traditions*. Traditions, or denominational "distinctives," are what make the Body of Christ rich and interesting. These traditions make it a diverse body instead of a single-celled amoeba. All of us are a part of some sort of faith tradition. Some might think their church is completely nontraditional, but even in that non-traditionalism, a tradition has been established. These are the distinctives that are true for your group, things that make your group unique from other groups. They don't make you right; they make you different. Southern Baptists aren't better than United Methodists, but the two groups are distinct, theologically and socially. Most importantly, both of them are orthodox. They believe in the essentials and are therefore true followers of the Jesus of the Bible.

I have been a part of a movement of churches since it began some years ago. This movement is unique in several ways—perhaps most significantly in its worship and its approach to outreach. I have many Methodist and Baptist friends who would feel they were being tortured if they were forced to sit through a Vineyard service and miss their traditional hymns on a Sunday. One older pastor friend of mine has told me he hopes he is not placed in heaven anywhere near the people of my movement. If he were, he would be tortured by what we call worship! Preferences don't make one style right and another wrong. It makes each different and unique. Having been a Christian for more than 30 years, I've been exposed to a vast diversity of styles of worship. I don't understand all of them, but I appreciate all of them because they are nurturing various parts of the Church.

Last, there are *Opinions*. The essentials form a very small circle since there are just a few things that we must believe to be authentic Christians. The traditions form a significantly larger circle; we have more traditions that have developed over the years. But by far the largest circle is formed by our opinions. The longer we spend in the Christian life, the more we accumulate opinions. Some of our opinion gathering is helpful.

But we've all come to plenty of opinions that aren't all that helpful to us or anyone else. Unfortunately, we often hold to those opinions fiercely.

Examples of topics where opinions cluster are liberation theology, ecology, nuclear power, gun control, eschatology (the end times), and the role of women in ministry.

Throughout church history, leaders have gotten in trouble for making their opinions public in inappropriate settings. Martin Luther made infamous anti-Semitic statements that were recorded in his Table Talk books. Luther had been drinking heavily when he said odd things that were recorded by others sitting at his table at taverns. Luther and Calvin split from each other over the meaning of the Lord's Supper.

I have hundreds of opinions that I choose to not make part of my tradition nor part of my list of essentials. I typically don't bring these opinions up when I teach or preach. No doubt if you and I were to sit down over a cup of coffee and talk long enough about our various opinions, we would eventually come to a place of disagreement. These are issues we've both thought through for a long time, and we each have good reason to hold those opinions. But that doesn't keep us from being Christians on the same mission.

When it comes to my inner circle of pastoral friends, I don't see eye to eye on numbers of issues, in the opinions category especially. Even though I have been a devoted and studious follower of Jesus for many decades now, I still find myself engaging in conversations that are invigorating and helpful with friends who have thought through issues from a different perspective than me. I have been persuaded to change my opinion many times in recent years on even longstanding matters. But we don't necessarily see eye to eye on all theological issues when it comes to the opinions category. That's okay, because we are close enough on the important issues, those things that fill in the essentials rubric.

It is important to keep these circles in mind: a small one that is vital; a larger one that is negotiable; a vast one that is worth chatting about over a cup of coffee sometime.

Fighting between brothers and sisters is perpetuated when they forget the order of the circles. It happens when I make tradition essential instead of negotiable. Or, worse yet, it happens when I consider my opinion about a topic to be an essential. These dyslexic episodes must grieve the heart of God. When He has vital work for the church to be about, we have sometimes been found arguing about absolutely non-vital matters.

What Is Essential?

Who Jesus Is

Perhaps there is really just one essential question. If we are talking about the same Jesus—the Jesus as revealed in the Scriptures—then we are on common ground and are brothers. Jesus is the beginning, the middle and the end of all discussions about orthodoxy.

Have you ever spoken with people in cultic groups who are trying to pass themselves off as Christian? Or have you talked about beliefs with conservative evangelicals with pseudo-Christian groups such as Mormons, who will readily say that they believe in Jesus as the Son of God? They'll say they believe that He is the way, the truth, and the life and that no one gets to the Father but by Him. But there's a catch. They're not talking about the unique Son of God—the one of a kind, capital S Son of God who was fully God and fully man at the same time. They aren't even talking about the same Father, for that matter. Like members of cults, conservative evangelicals sometimes seek to explain away all the mystery of God with manmade analogies. We must be careful that Christians hold the essential belief that separates us from all of the cults: namely, that Jesus is God in the flesh. What's essential is that people are worshiping Jesus Christ as He is revealed in the Bible.

For a good study on the biblical Christ versus some of the imposter Christs that are commonly posed by the cults, I suggest reading *Kingdom of the Cults* by Walter Martin. He goes into great depth regarding the orthodox view of the Trinity and the Godhead. This is a worthwhile book to add to your library.

Where We Get Our Truth

We confine our search for truth to the pages of Scripture. Like Luther's, our conscience is held captive to the pages of the Scriptures. They are our guide to all moral questions. The Scripture is our source for inspired wisdom in life. It reveals the knowledge of God to us. It is the revelation of God's character and nature. Without it we would have no clear light or knowledge of God in this world.

How We Get Right with God

It is essential that we see that we are lost in our sins because of our connection to our ancestors Adam and Eve. We are part of a lost race: the human race. We were born into sin and separated from God at birth. Before coming to Christ, all of us were spiritually blind and incapable of finding our way to God on our own. God, in His mercy and grace, made Himself known to each of us in numerous ways by the working of the Holy Spirit in our lives. In short, He opens our eyes to our need for salvation.

> There is tremendous spiritual confusion in our current culture. Many don't know their left hand from their right, spiritually speaking. An ad that promotes Deepak Chopra's book *How to Know God* says, "You don't have to believe in God to experience God."

We must repent, turn our lives over to the control of Christ and put our future in His hands. We must believe that His death on the cross was on our behalf. When we ask God to apply upon our lives the sacrificial blood of Jesus that was shed for us on the cross, we are, at that moment, made right with God. Our deep inner spiritual hunger is quenched only when we finally relinquish control of our lives to Jesus. In so giving our lives over to Him, we, for the first time, experience the peace of God that surpasses understanding. It is that peace that we were designed to walk in.

Some see this entire action as a covenant that we enter during childhood, while others (myself included) view this as a process that takes place in each person's heart at some point after they reach an age of accountability. As long as each person has repented and placed his or her faith in Christ, we are in the same boat.

True: What Is Tradition?

In my observations, all growing and thriving churches are low on the scale of the tradition they come out of. You've probably heard of "Low Catholic." That means the church conducts mass in English (not Latin), guitars replace the pipe organ, and the priest speaks in understandable and user-friendly language.

There is a low version of church in every denomination. For example, I describe my church as being "Low Vineyard." By definition, there are also "High Vineyard" churches where services are quite different from what we are doing in north Cincinnati. By "Low Vineyard," I mean that we worship for just 20 minutes. We have a quick and efficient couple of "plugs" (we don't have announcements). Our message is 30 minutes long typically, and we are done in 60 minutes total. We're pretty efficient. In and out—no one gets hurt.

In virtually every denomination, the high version is not growing. I am not aware of a move on the part of any who are looking for a tradition to join. People are looking for life, honesty and authenticity. The high versions of church, no matter what their flavor, just don't sell to our postmodern culture that places such a high value on "realness." As one pastor friend of mine says of his own denomination:

Some assembly of God
may be required.

True:
What Are Opinions?

Throughout my years of doing servant evangelism projects, I have had many conversations with not-yet-believers who were trying to figure out the Christian faith. The questions they ask me tend to be very similar. Conversations often go something like this:

"There are so many versions of the Bible. I wouldn't know which one to pick up even if I were to begin to read it."

"You want to read a big black Bible."

"There's so much in the Bible that I find confusing and contradictory. I just don't know."

"Which part don't you understand?"

"All of it."

"But what part have you read that gives you trouble?"

"Well, I actually haven't read any of it."

"Why don't you begin to read the book of John, and we'll talk through the parts that you don't understand."

Another conversation I've had several times is a reflection of our times:

"You know the Bible? Well, I think, like, people didn't write it. But, like, a long time ago, aliens brought the Bible here and dropped it off on earth as a book to, like, help us learn how to get along with each other. That's what I think."

"Well, if that's true, like, don't you think that, if aliens went to all that trouble to come across the universe, you ought to at least read it?"

Usually they say, "Well, like, I guess so."

> **How to Become More True**
>
> Ask yourself the following questions:
>
> • Are your *Essentials* the same as those laid out in this chapter?
> • What does your list of *Traditions* look like?
> • Are your *Opinions* out of control?

Chapter 12

COOPERATIVE

As the woman worked in her garden,

her not-yet-believer neighbor approached her. He asked, "Are you a member of the big church?"

Earlier that day the woman had been a part of a citywide event in her hometown of Abbotsford, British Columbia, near Vancouver in western Canada. Christians in this city of about one hundred thousand began an experiment a couple of years ago. They banded together to serve their city in large-scale, creative and profound ways. I have been privileged to be a part of training those who do outreach. It is always exciting to train motivated people.

At the last event they held, which they dubbed Love Abbotsford, some 1,400 people from 30 local churches came out for various serving projects around the city. Everyone wore a white T-shirt with a large heart on it and handed out cards to explain the projects. The cards didn't promote individual churches but the "big C" church in the city. The cards named the Love Abbotsford event and referred people to a shared website that explained the entire project. The day went smoothly. Many thousands of people were touched, and the participants came back enthused.

Now back to the woman working in her garden that afternoon. Her not-yet-Christian neighbor stopped by and asked, "Say, I was in town today and saw all the folks with T-shirts. Are you a part of the big church with the T-shirts?"

She thought for a second about her church, which had several hundred people. "Well, my church is pretty big."

The neighbor said, "No, the *really* big church, the one with the hundreds of people who were out on the town today—*that* church." She got it. Her heart was touched, she teared up, and she said, "Yes, in fact, I am a part of the big church!"

God is busy building the big church these days. If we are going to be a great church, we need to be larger than a small, single church. God has much for us to accomplish. We'll reach our potential only as we team up with the larger church.

I've been doing some dreaming. Dream with me for a bit.

What if . . . we realized the truth that we can't reach our city by ourselves, even if our church is relatively large and well-equipped? We need an army made up of the various churches around our city. No matter what the set-up is in our city or our individual church, we still need the whole kit and caboodle of the church. We cannot thrive in the big picture without the church of Jesus coming together to work as one force in the city.

What if . . . we were willing to cooperate with other churches, even churches that don't necessarily hold all the same traditions and opinions that we do? What if we were willing to co-operate in times like these in which the perfect picture of a unified church will never be seen? The picture many are looking for is really more of a notion of ease that doesn't require any digging or discussion on the parts of leaders.

What if . . . we prayed each weekend that God would bless the churches of the city first before He blessed our church—and we meant it? A good start would be something like this: "God, bless Your church in this city with Your presence, in a significant way. And once You've blessed the other churches who love You, then come and visit us with Your presence as well."

What if . . . we really got along? The unchurched have no idea why we can't get along. People who don't go to church are extremely put off by churches that are in competition with one another. At a recent food giveaway, a fellow stepped into our ministry bus and said, "I can't believe it!"

We said, "What, sir? We're just giving away food."

"I just can't believe it," he continued.

"What is it that you can't believe?"

"I've been on your church bus four times, and I haven't seen your church name anywhere on it—I can't believe it!"

There's a hunger in the unchurched world to see the church do altruistic things, and there's a double hunger for the same in the membership of the church.

What if . . . we looked out for one another in the church scene? If one church gets a good name, we will all benefit from it; if one church gets a bad name, we will all suffer for it. It only makes sense that we begin to take seriously the reputation of the entire church in the city.

What if . . . God doesn't see us as being in different churches? What if God just sees those people who don't belong to His vast Church? It doesn't make sense to view our relationships as competitive. Thus, we need to seek the people who are not connected with any church. If we did this, the sense of any aspect of competition would go out the window immediately. There are thousands of those folks nearby you who are just waiting for a touch from God. You are their gateway into the life of God. Let's stop every bit of energy we've been investing in focusing on the differences between us and let's see if we can come close to downright promoting one another in the city God has placed us in. Are you boundlessly excited about the work of God that is going on in the churches around your city?

What if . . . we came alongside other people's dreams and blessed those dreams? When we include other people, we join ourselves to their dream. In most churches, the idea of "coming alongside someone" is an unwelcome idea—it sounds intrusive. That isn't what I'm talking about. I'm talking about the sorts of things that make everybody happy. This is the idea of connecting at the deepest level of spirituality.

What if . . . we saw our wellbeing interwoven with the wellbeing of other churches in the city? We have a city-reaching perspective that requires the help of the entire church if we are to succeed. We will never accomplish much if our goal is to stop at the boundaries of our church. For example, why not take offerings for other churches as the need presents itself? Churches that take offerings for other churches are churches with a great destiny. That sort of behavior is rare, but it would be great if churches became self-actualized enough to think beyond themselves.

What if . . . we lived out the truth that it really is better to give than to receive?

A while back in Cincinnati, 200 churches gathered together to reach out to a large portion of the city in an afternoon. After much planning and dreaming, we combined efforts to reach out and touch more than 300,000 people in a matter of a couple of hours. Instead of promoting one church over another, all the churches used the same connection card. They simply explained that the project was something that showed God's love in a practical way and referenced the day of serving the city as the sponsor of the act of kindness.

Billboards throughout the city advertised that simple website address with a hand-engraved heart. We gave away bottles of water. The event was so popular that we were *the* news event of the weekend locally. We connected it with the next day's Billy Graham Mission that was about to take place. The outreach empowered the churchgoers of the city in their outwardness.

When it was finished, the words of Ronald Reagan came to mind: "When no one cares who gets the credit, a lot of good can happen."

"Are you from the Big Church?" I hope so, for that is the future. Active membership in the Big Church is what the Holy Spirit wants for your church today.

Chapter 13

LEADING OUT

> *Draw, Antonio, and do not waste time.*
> Michelangelo

No one had started a new church in Chilocothe (CHILL-o-caw-thee) in decades. This medium-sized town located in central Ohio just wasn't on many church planters' most-admired-cities list. Just the same, my friend Steve Goode felt called to launch a new church there. But how do you start something in a town that has zero church-planting momentum? How do you get going when no one is inviting you to come?

Steve launched out in a small way: He and his wife began by giving away coffee at local Friday night high school football games. They were there game after game on cold evenings to help people ward off the chill. It wasn't long before curious individuals asked Steve what in the world he was doing at these cold games every week. Soon these strangers became friends and joined him in his outreaches. With a handful of people, he had a glimmer of momentum. Those people joined his first home group. The plan was simple: to meet in small groups to learn to love one another and then do an excellent job of reaching out into the community in practical ways.

Today, the small group of coffee distributors has mushroomed to more than 500 people each weekend. They are still going out into the community each week doing a variety of outward-focused projects, and they are helping to plant other churches in their area. The church is becoming a great church by all accounts. That's what I call outward-facing leadership.

Which Direction Are You Facing?

All leaders are aimed in some direction. We are looking mainly toward the inward or mainly toward the outward side of things. The question is, are we preoccupied with who is already here and the never-ending series of problems those people bring with them or are we aimed at the issues the not-yet-connected people usher in? It's a matter of growing or not growing, moving forward or stagnating. It is easy to fixate on the already-gathered and stay busy for the rest of our lives with those already-connected people. We can defend those people's issues as sufficient for the rest of our lives. But is that what we really are called to for the rest of our lives as leaders who are working with them? The easy answer is that we are certainly not called to the current time frame forever. We are called to move forward always. We are called to intermingle our times with all those nearby.

If I find someone who is an expert at building disciples, I make it a priority to have that person *do* things with people, not just *teach* people new things. Being a disciple isn't primarily about going to church, praying and reading the Bible. Being a disciple means doing the deeds that Jesus did.

We don't expect our people to feel a certain something or express a certain emotion but to develop certain behaviors. Even if I am in a bad mood, I can still rake a leaf or wash a car. In the first two years of discipleship—both for individuals and for new churches—we establish the rudiments of doing rather than just talking. Once that's established in our hearts, we will do it and teach our friends about it.

We must be the sort of people who lead outward continually. Scripture calls us to lead out: "Therefore go and make disciples" (Matt. 28:19). We live in the age of "Go," according to the calling of God upon the church. If we are to obey, we can only be the church that leads out instead of in.

We can lead out in a number of ways.

Lead Out by Being Decisive

Right now, more than at any other time, the church needs leaders who know where they are going. We don't need to make rash decisions; we simply need to make decisions that are carefully considered and—once seen clearly—courageously acted upon. Courage is a commodity that leadership circles always need more of.

Lead Out by Taking Bold Risks

How does your leadership team deal with failure? Think of the way embarrassment and understanding come together when a "mistake" is made.

What's most typical is *high embarrassment* accompanied with *low understanding*. The church is known for shaming and blaming when mistakes are made. What if we inverted that arrangement so that when things went wrong people experienced *low embarrassment* accompanied with *high understanding*? How much further ahead would we be if, when things went wrong, they weren't viewed as errors as much as they were seen as learning experiences that propel us forward?

Ready, Fire! Aim

I am best known for the large church that I planted some years ago in Cincinnati. I've also been very involved in helping

Take a Chance

Did I ever tell you about the young Zode,
Who came to two signs at the fork of the road?
One said, "To Place One," and the other, "Place Two."
So the Zode had to make up his mind what to do.
Well . . . the Zode scratched his head. And his chin. And his pants.
And he said to himself, "I'll be taking a chance.
If I go to Place One, now that place may be hot!
So how do I know if I'll like it or not?
On the other hand, though I'll sort of be a fool,
If I go to Place Two, I might find it too cool.
In that case, I may catch a chill and turn blue!
On the other hand, though, if Place One is too high,
I may catch a terrible earache and die!
So Place Two may be the best!
On the other hand, though . . .
What might happen to me if Place Two is too low?
I might get some strange pain in my toe!"
Then he said, "On the other hand, though . . .
On the other hand, though . . . On the other hand, though . . ."
And for thirty-six and one-half hours, that poor Zode
Made starts and stops at the fork in the road,
Saying, "Don't take a chance, you may not be right."
Then he got an idea that was wonderfully bright!
"Play safe!" cried the Zode. "I'll play safe! I'm no dunce!
I'll simply start off for both places at once!"
And that's how the Zode, who would not take a chance,
Got no place at all, with a split in his pants.

AUTHOR UNKNOWN

lots of other people start churches. But what many people don't know is that I don't see the same results with every church plant I'm involved with. Every year I step out to coach the planting of a number of new churches. Every year some make it and some don't do nearly as well. I always start out thinking that every new church will excel. I'm always somewhat surprised and very disappointed when a church doesn't make it in a spectacular way. I honestly can't tell the difference between the startup that ends up doing extremely well and the one that doesn't do so well. They look almost identical on paper.

When I talk to the leaders, they seem to be essentially identical. No one is withholding information from me. There are just a lot of odd factors that I cannot take into consideration easily—let's call them the "God factors" that are beyond our reckoning. There are things that are out of our control. We pray with fervency. We plan with great dependence upon the Holy Spirit's power. We work toward the end that God will show up and do amazing things in our midst, and we work until our fingers are bleeding. But in the end, the results are out of our control. Our role is to continue to risk boldly. If we stop that, we are in big trouble. God calls us to rely strongly upon Him.

Church planting is a lot like the old Wild West. There are gunslingers galore. There is gunfire. People are being shot and some are even dying as result of being hit. We'll all end up losing our lives in the end, but in our case, for a good cause—a cause that matters supremely. My guess is that there's a lot more spiritual activity going on than we realize when it comes to extending God's kingdom. We don't quite understand all the ramifications of what is going on around us but there is certainly a lot of activity that is going on between light and darkness. We tend to be oblivious to this warfare and we can probably all stand to pray a lot more for our benefit and for that of our churches. One thing is clear: We must continue to take giant-sized risks that lean heavily into the power and presence of the God of the universe. For His sake and for the sake of the love of Jesus that we spread abroad, we must do this by all opportunities afforded to us.

Worth Living and Dying For

Two of the passengers on Alaska Airlines Flight 261 that crashed en route from Mexico to Seattle in January 2000 were Linda and Joe Knight. These co-pastors of Rock Church in Monroe, Washington, had been in Puerto Vallarta, Mexico, working with children who live in the city dumps. After their deaths, their work was continued as a memorial to them in the form of a community center. This new center is complete with a community shower, a medical clinic, and a dining area for the children of about 200 families who live in the filth and poverty of the shanties and lean-tos of the dump city. That center was dedicated on February 15, 2001. They were risk-takers par excellence.[1]

Lead Out by Taking the Lead Yourself

Ernest Shackleton was the leader of the crew of the *HMS Endurance*. The ship, a British scientific exploratory vessel, set sail from London just prior to the sudden beginning of World War I. When the ship became icebound near the South Pole, no one was able to come to the crew's aid. Finally it became apparent that no one was going to rescue them, and Ernest Shackleton changed his goal from traversing the Antarctic continent to saving the lives of his crew.

Eventually the ice crushed their ship; the crew was stuck with mere tents and several lifeboats. Ultimately they decided to send six men to try to reach a whaling station 800 miles away. Shackleton led the way, and the rescue party shoved off. Their venture was a huge gamble: the men had only a sextant and a hand compass to guide them across the most dangerous ocean in the world.

After 17 days at sea they made it to the island, but steep mountains and uncharted territory lay between them and rescue. Leaving three men in the cove with the boat, Shackleton led the other two men into the mountains, headed "magnetic East" toward a whaling station—they hoped. For 36 hours straight, the men climbed and slid. At one point, the way forward required jumping into a waterfall. Finally the party of three arrived at the whaling station. After a couple of days of recuperation, Shackleton led a rescue team back to the icebound crew. Not a single man of the *Endurance* crew was lost.

I have read a number of books about the voyage of the *Endurance*, and they all point to Shackleton's incredible activist leadership as the key to everyone's survival.[2]

His outstanding characteristics were his care of, and anxiety for, the lives and wellbeing of all his men.
Frank Worsley of Ernest Shackleton

Shackleton's outstanding quality was his penchant for being a leader who did what he talked about. He didn't direct a
rescue plan from the sidelines. He got into the middle of things.
He took risks along with his men. The crew respected him for
it and drew strength from his willingness to go forward regardless of fears he might have had. Shackleton's lead-by-doing approach was the key to the crew's survival against all odds in one
of the harshest environments imaginable.

Lead Out by Teaching Your People to Be Practical Doers

A dichotomy exists in the church between theoretical and
action-oriented Christianity. As you might guess, I am a big ad-
vocate of the practical, action side of things. I don't see great
value in increasing our list of theories. It seems to me that, if we
would simply apply the lengthy list of topics that we have all
learned over the past several years and stay away from more the-
ory, we would probably grow as a result.

The student-mystic role is what many new followers of
Christ are encouraged to achieve. However, that model of discipleship doesn't work and serves only to alienate new believers
from their old friends. A much better approach is to have new
followers make a commitment to spend time with the poor.

They can come to us in a variety of packages. They may be
our old friends who are looking for something more in life.
(That something more is Christ, as we know Him.) We are the
bridge between them and the One they need to know. The poor
can come to us in the package of the person next door who is
going through the breakdown of a relationship—perhaps their
marriage is falling apart and they are poor in spirit, especially
now. The poor can come to us in the form of people who are

depressed. Jesus said that the fields are white unto harvest. What does a head of grain look like when it is ripe and ready to be harvested? It is bent over and sags toward the ground a bit. It is not standing straight up as though everything is all right; it is bent down. Just so are people who are "ripe" and ready for their spiritual harvest bent down physically in their demeanor. They literally are bent over a bit. They are so burdened by life and by the emotions of things that are going on in their situation that their shoulders are humped over a bit. Those who are standing erect beside them with a smile on their faces are typically not ripe and ready for the spiritual harvest God is up to. By conversing with people who are "ripe," we can engage them in what might well be the most significant conversation of their entire life. We can engage them in a spiritual conversation concerning the way they can unburden themselves through a relationship with Christ and gain the eternal freedom that God alone offers.

Lead Out by Focusing Beyond Ourselves

Leadership is based on action, on doing, on serving. The term "deacon" is literally a "dust kicker": one who makes a dust cloud from his or her flurry of serving. This clarifies that God's intention from the beginning has been that the notion of leadership connected with people is seeing others as more important than ourselves. For this to happen, we must get our eyes off of ourselves. We have to get our attention off of the challenges that make up our lives. Of course we all have difficulties. We all are the descendents of Adam, and battling sin is our lot in life. That is true for every last one of us. But a lot of life is not so horrible that we cannot grow beyond that box. Our role in life is to be people of large hearts—so large, in fact, that we can encompass those around us easily, without stress. We connect with others by the power God supplies to us. He is the power that flows through us.

Outwardly Focused People

We are going for it, for life is short.

The day after the September 11, 2001, bombing of the World Trade Center buildings, our entire staff of over 100 piled into buses and went to downtown Cincinnati's highest point, the top of the Carew Tower. There we prayed for our nation and our city for an extended time. As we prayed individually, I found myself asking God to make our lives count. With the fresh shock of September 11 in my mind, I couldn't help but think that life is short and unpredictable.

If what we are calling "ministry" isn't generating changed lives, then we need to seriously examine how much time we are spending in planning versus doing.

Leading Destiny

There is always an enormous temptation in all of life to diddle around making itsy-bitsy friends and meals and journeys for itsy-bitsy years on end. It is so self-conscious, so apparently moral. . . . I won't have it. The world is wilder than that in all directions, more dangerous and bitter, more extravagant and bright. We are making hay when we should be making whoopee; we are raising tomatoes when we should be raising Cain, or Lazarus.[3]

Let's lead out and develop some great churches that are committed to being what God wants them to be in this broken, needy but highly receptive world He has placed us in.

Notes

1. Caroline Alexander, *The Endurance* (New York: Alfred A. Knopf, 1999).
2. Ibid.
3. Annie Dillard, *Three by Annie Dillard* (New York: HarperCollins, 1990), p. 258.

Want to jumpstart outreach in your church?

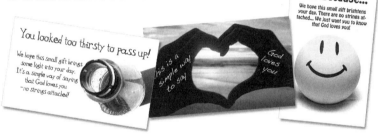

ALSO BY
STEVE SJOGREN

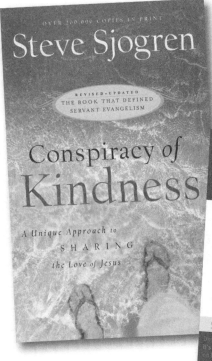

Conspiracy of Kindness
ISBN 978.08307.45722
ISBN 08307.45726

Community of Kindness
ISBN 978.08307.29722
ISBN 08307.29720

Available at Bookstores Everywhere!

Visit **www.regalbooks.com** to join **Regal's FREE e-newsletter.**
You'll get useful **excerpts** from our newest releases and **special
access to online chats with your favorite authors.** Sign up today!

God's Word for Your World™
www.regalbooks.com